Cops don't cry:

My story of PTSD and Resiliency

Jason Rorick

Copyright © 2020 Jason Rorick

All rights reserved

The characters and events portrayed in this book are fictitious. Any similarity to real persons, living or dead, is coincidental and not intended by the author.

No part of this book may be reproduced, or stored in a retrieval system, or transmitted in any form or by any means, electronic, mechanical, photocopying, recording, or otherwise, without express written permission of the publisher.

ISBN- 9798582029991

Cover design by: Daniel Sundahl

Preface

Have you ever wondered if you were the only one struggling with an issue? Feeling like you were forced to suffer in silence, either fearing you would harm your reputation from those you told, or unable to over come your feeling of embarrassment to let others know what is going on?

Especially when it come to psychological injuries many suffer alone, with feelings of guilt, or feeling of pride that they will push through and be better. This book offers insight into my journey, from the beginning where my major dream was to become a police officer, when I achieved that goal and began suffering from the traumatic events I had witnessed, I felt trapped, alone, and unsure what to do.

When it finally became darkest, I swallowed my pride and asked for help, I had no idea what brand new world would await me, not only would I return to work, but I would return to work healthier than I had ever been, and found a joy at work I could only imagine.

I was armed with the skills to continue to work in a job where exposure to traumatic situations is normal, without having those exposures negatively impact my life.

This book will take you through that journey, and will share my thought process through each situation. You will understand how easy it is to ignore or justify signs and symptoms. You will get to witness from my first hand account how the proper treatment, and proper strategies allow a person to return to the work they love, and have a great time doing it.

This book follows me from my humble beginnings, right up to my current life at the time of writing this book.

Contents

Title Page	1
Copyright	2
Preface	3
Chapter One - Childhood Dreams	7
Chapter Two - Time to Grow Up	25
Chapter Three - Still Haven't Grown Up	36
Chapter Four - A Dream Life	47
Chapter Five - When Dreams Become Reality	61
Chapter Six - When Dreams Become Nightmares	75
Chapter Seven - Getting Help	88
Chapter Eight - Aftermath	100
About The Author	113

Chapter One - Childhood Dreams

My story begins in Cranbrook, British Columbia, the first place that I remember growing up. I was born in Nelson, which is also located in BC, but my memories of childhood begin in Cranbrook. Like many other children I became fascinated with the idea of being a police officer. That was the answer I gave when asked what I wanted to be for my school's year-end book in kindergarten. As I grew older, that desire became stronger and stronger. At around nine years old, I was given a notebook as a present and combined with a pen I had a summer filled with fun. I was pretty self-sufficient and although I had two brothers, I often found myself playing alone, most of the time riding my bike around the neighbourhood. However, that summer would be a little different. In addition to riding my bike, I had a notepad and paper with which to write down all suspicious vehicle licence plates that I could find. Now I have to admit, that at that age everything appeared suspicious, as far as I was concerned. If you didn't park exactly inside the lines, you were going into my notebook. If your car had a little damage, well you guessed it, I was going to record your plate in my book. I remember spending hours and hours just riding around on my bike, looking for these suspect plates so that I could write them down. When I found a vehicle where anything was out of the ordinary, I stopped my bike, pulled in behind the vehicle, and wrote down the plate's details. I also wrote down a description of the 'suspicious' activity with which the vehicle was associated. Now of course I never did anything with the book, I just wrote down things that summer, and never saw it again and even though there was nothing criminal recorded, it provides some great insight into my personality. Of all the policing activities things to get excited about, such as driving fast, arresting criminals, having lights and sirens, I was interested in writing down license plates and documenting information. If only I'd known at that time how much police preparation I was getting. At around the same age, besides doing regular kid stuff like playing on the jungle gym and causing shenanigans with my brothers, I was developing a love for martial arts.

At the age of ten, I was enrolled in Taekwondo classes that were held at the local school gym close to my house. I immediately loved the sport. I got to jump and I got to kick. What ten-year-old boy wouldn't love that? We had a very large club and would constantly break off into little groups, forming a circle in order to work the martial arts techniques with several different partners. One evening, we were working in our groups on a jumping front kick. The aim of the exercise was to perform the kick close to the person you were working with without hitting them. The drill involved each person taking their fighting stance and squaring off with one person at a time, until they'd practiced the drill with everyone in their group. My cousin, who was eight years older than me and was the senior student in the class, was in my group. When the time came for me to work with him, his kick got a little too close and hit my thumb. Everyone in the group stopped what they were doing, while the instructor immediately rushed over to make sure I was okay. I can't remember all the exact details of the conversation, but do clearly recall him asking me if I was about to cry. I was quite offended at the suggestion and quickly replied that I didn't cry. Even though by then my thumb had swollen to about three times its normal size, I shook off the injury. I simply went back to working on the drills, because hey, I didn't cry.

Shortly after this incident, my Taekwondo career would come to an end when my family moved to Creston, BC. My family included my mom, my older brother, Gerry, and younger brother, Justin. My dad had left when I was four years old. I can't say I have or had any memories of him, except of him never being there. When we moved to

Creston, I continued with my love of policing and my ambition to one day become a police officer. Of course, this still involved the non-traditional police activities that children my age were often fascinated with. I loved all aspects of policing, not just the highlight reel activities that would make news coverage. I remember watching a documentary about an awesome program called CPIC, in which you could punch in a vehicle's plate details and get all this information about the vehicle and the driver, just from a license plate. I'd spend lunch hours and recesses telling the kids in my class with endless enthusiasm about all the wonderful things CPIC could do. My friends listened and I can only imagine what they thought as I went on for hours about the program. CPIC only became operational in 1972, in a time where the was no internet, information was harder to come by, and in 1989 CPIC wasn't well known by most adults and most certainly not by ten-year-old children.

Over the next few years, every time I saw a police car drive by, I watched in awe. I hung on every word as Gerry's friend talked about his time as an RCMP auxiliary officer. Then in grade seven I had one of my most memorable experiences with the police. It was another day at school, or so I thought. The day was ending and my excitement growing then came the afterschool announcements, which normally indicated that school was done. The announcement stated that two people had illegally entered Canada at the border crossing just outside Creston and were now in the town. There was concern that they might attempt to take a school bus filled with children. Consequently, we'd all be staying an hour later than usual and the bus schedules were altered. If, like me, children didn't take the bus, they could walk home but had to be there with an adult. I knew that I wouldn't be able to go home, as my mom had to work three jobs and wouldn't be back until late that evening. However, my grandfather lived right across the street from our house.

I walked home very cautiously, watching every vehicle, every person, trying to take some obscure routes off the beaten track. I arrived at my grandfather's and noticed my brother Justin had gone home after school, as I could see him in the driveway heading towards the house, from my grandfather's place. I yelled from outside my Grandfather's house at him to get over to our grandfather's house right away. As the story came out through teachers, as well as the local newspaper I was fascinated by the events. Two men from the United States had robbed an armoury, pulled up to the Canadian border in a vehicle, got out of the vehicle and then locked the guards in a closet at gunpoint. At that time Canadian border guards weren't armed. After locking up the guards the suspects got back in their vehicle, crossed the border in Canada, and then headed towards Creston, BC. A person looking to return to Canada had waited at the border for a very long time, before deciding to go inside the building were the border guards were stationed and see what was taking so long, finding the guards locked in the closet. The guards immediately called the RCMP, who found the vehicle outside of the school I'd attended until grade six. Both occupants ran and a female RCMP officer tackled one of the guys and had taken him into custody. The other man got away and they were searching for him. By the next day the man had been found and arrested. It was scary, as he'd kicked in the door of a home that was located only two houses away from where one of my good friends lived. They found the man with a gas mask, tear gas, tears gas launchers, and grenades. I was inspired by how quickly the two men had been apprehended, along with the bravery of the officer that confronted the two criminals by herself and took one of them into custody. I also thought a lot about how scary it must have been for the border guards and how important it was that the person who found them was able to recognize there was a problem and investigate. I felt extremely proud of how quickly the RCMP had acted in getting information to the schools and apprehending the two individuals before they could cause any harm in our community.

After an exciting grade seven school year, it was time to start high school, which went from grade eight until grade twelve. For any young man without a lot of confidence, high school can be a very challenging place. I found myself being challenged fairly regularly, trying to determine which groups I might fit into. I had a good size group of friends that I'd known and been friends with since the end of grade four, beginning of grade five, but always felt a little on the outside with most of them. They all had fathers, a parent that talked to them about fighting, dealing with bullies, and all those things fathers talked to their sons about. All my friends seemed to have both their parents in their lives, had a lot more money than my family, and therefore had a lot more things than I did. I often felt like the kid who had nothing. Most of my clothes were hand-me-downs and I only got a haircut when my grandfather was tired of my scraggly hair. I never went on vacations over the summer and was unable to contribute to many conversations with those friends. All of them had at least one vehicle that their family owned, while my family didn't. My friends all showed up to school in brand new clothes, with brand new shoes. I showed up in my second-hand clothes, shirts I'd worn since grade four, and in very basic shoes, not the fancy basketball types they could all afford. I wasn't underclothed or deprived, just not able to have the expensive clothes or shoes that all my friends could afford. My friends never made fun of my situation or made me feel bad. I just felt inside that I wasn't as good as they were because I didn't have those things. I sometimes didn't understand how it was fair that if I wanted the same shoes that they had, I had to work so hard at my paper route and save for so long.

A personality trait that grew stronger in high school was my sense of fair play and fairness. Sometimes I'd see older kids picking on younger kids, on other occasions bigger kids picking on weaker kids. Before high school, the major thing the grade sevens talked about was what grade eight would be like and what kind of bullying the older kids were going to do to us. We'd all heard stories of the types of bullying that went on there. We heard of the grease lines, where the older kids would line up on either side of a hallway and push a younger kid that was trying to walk by, back and forth until they reached the end of the line. I often found myself wondering why this happened. Why did older and bigger kids have to pick on younger, smaller kids? Why couldn't they just get along with one another? I'd also wonder why the kids getting picked on didn't fight back, or why no one ever seemed to step in. Even if they weren't going to win, why not at least stand up for yourself and say hey, I don't accept this? There were many times when I'd step in by alerting a teacher, and at least for the moment, the problem ended. I also did my best to avoid such situations personally, since I wasn't very big and lacked self-confidence. My rule was not to get personally involved, unless I was forced into the situation.

However, there was one huge exception to this rule, which was that you didn't mess with my family. No one picked on my younger brother or older brother without having to deal with me. One summer, this lead to a situation when my older brother and I were walking past the high school, where a large group of high school kids and skateboarders were sitting around the front entrance.

"What are you looking at?" one kid shouted.

"Nothing special," my brother replied.

We continued walking toward downtown when we noticed that the entire group was following us on their skateboards. There were between fifteen and twenty of them and only two of us. Yet even though we were heavily outnumbered, I was fearless, thinking that I'd fight everyone and anyone to make sure no one hurt my family. However, my brother just wouldn't allow me to get involved. The situation ended when he pushed the leader of the group and they realized he was going to fight back. My brother was always bigger than his classmates and several of the kids that were older. Despite this, my brother didn't often fight back for himself, but just like me, he was going to protect his family.

There was one other time I remember when I couldn't sit back any longer and allow injustice to happen. I saw a kid roller-skating with his dog, which ran in front of him and tripped the boy with the leash. The kid then started wailing on the dog, using an open fist, a closed fist, and just continuing, with no sign of stopping. I walked over and punched him in the stomach, telling him to stop hitting the dog. This ended up being one of my first significant lessons in learning to use words first. Had I just used my words with this kid, used language designed to gain compliance and have him stop hitting the dog, without me hitting him, I'd have saved myself a lot of grief. When this kid went home and told his dad what had happened, I suspect without the part of him hitting the dog in the head, his dad decided to find me. I'd taken mostly the back alleys home as I usually did, and had just arrived in the parking lot beside the 7 Eleven, on the main road of town, when he saw me and slammed on his brakes. I can still hear the screeching tires in my mind to this day. He pulled into the parking lot and chased me around in his vehicle, seeming like he was going to hit me with the car. He never did, only asking for an apology for his son, and rightfully so. I realize now that there were many other options for me to have defended the dog without using force. This included grabbing his hand to prevent any more strikes to just plain talking, but I guess that's why we refer to life as growing up. Other than those two situations, I was just left with a bunch of questions. Why wouldn't I put myself in danger to prevent those other kids from being picked on? I knew it was wrong and always did what I could to intervene, like alerting the teachers, and if I were in the situation myself I'd fight back

Grade eight and nine were very challenging years in my academic life. I was questioning myself regarding not putting myself in harm's way to protect the kids from being bullied. I started to feel embarrassed about being so weak. There was a lot of teasing at home, since I was the proverbial runt of the family. My brothers always called me wee wooden Willy, referencing my small stature. In hindsight I really was tiny and even by the end of high school I was never more than 155 pounds, even when six feet tall. My insecurities about not being able to have nice things, not going on summer vacations, or not having a vehicle, all added to me feeling as less than, rather than equal to, the people around me. All these questions I had about where I might fit in began to overwhelm me. I began to take on the role of class clown, constantly telling myself I was dumb. Not surprisingly, I started getting kicked out of classes and failing them. In grade nine I failed three classes and barely passed the other ones. Some days I'd avoid school, staying home to eat taco-flavoured beef and watch *Columbo* on television. Yes, police shows continued to be my favourites, although *The Legend of Kung Fu* rated right up there, whether it was fictional shows like *The Rockford Files* or *Columbo,* where they did police-like activities, or realistic shows like COPS, I enjoyed them catching the bad guy. My school life was just not going very well. Something had to change and my mother knew it. She'd tried to get me back into martial arts. There was a Taekwondo studio just up the hill from our place, within walking distance. She thought maybe that would be the answer, or perhaps she was tired of me constantly talking about martial arts. When she inquired about the price she quickly realized that this martial art school wasn't going to be the answer. There was no way we could have afforded that. She didn't have disposable cash to put me into activities like Taekwondo and my paper route couldn't provide enough income for me to pay for that. Yet just before the start of grade ten, we found the answer.

A non-profit Kempo Karate club was held at one of the elementary schools in the town, and I could walk to the class. The club's fees were only $25 per month. My paper route could easily support that. I had a very large route and when I stopped doing it, the route was split into three separate ones. I paid for my karate every month, even saving up to buy some extra equipment such a gi, a bojutsu, and tonfas. I felt I had to buy the tonfas because they were the martial art version of the police nightstick, which was one of the tools carried by police on their duty belts at that time. You might have guessed it, the day I bought those, and began to learn how to use them, my friends and family got to listen for many hours, as I explained how the police were just using traditional martial art weapons. The square tonfas I had were the proper weapon, while the rounded ones the police used where the variation. I found it so interesting that the tactics and tools that police officers used were all based on martial arts, like the one I was then doing. I loved

Kempo Karate, not because I thought it would get me a job as a police officer, but simply because I loved it. I felt like I fit in, that I was challenged and learning to defend myself, and also that with great power comes great responsibility. The more proficient we are at defending ourselves, the greater chance we have to hurt someone, so the greater responsibility we have to not engage in fights unless absolutely necessary. I knew that if I were forced to fight it was also important to use the lowest possible level of force. I was taught to 'show mercy on your enemy today, make a friend of him tomorrow', learning how not to use the techniques just as much as I was learning how to use them. This is sometimes referred to as the dragon or wisdom of martial arts. I was realizing that karate was the answer.

When I say it was the answer, I truly mean that. It would be a solution to many things later in my life, things that I had no way of knowing at the time. All I knew is that I loved going to the classes, working hard, gaining skills, and having my achievements recognized by being awarded belts. I went to all the extra sessions, including the Thursday night fight class. All we did at that one was sparring. The instructor always liked to say we were to train with 50 percent speed and power, but I can't recall a time with anything less than 80 percent speed or power. We wore full headgear, boxing gloves, and footpads. The instructor would bring in two large black garbage bags, dump them out, and we'd all race over to get our gear. I was often the only teenager in a group of adults, but I quickly established myself as a force to be reckoned with. I was only a yellow belt at the time but I did not know the meaning of retreat. I moved in one direction and one direction only, which was forward. This included sparring with my black belt instructor. I continued to come forward no matter what he hit me with, determined to find an answer and a way to win. The first time I moved in too fast for him to pull back his kick and got a full front push kick, right in the solar plexus. This is a kick down with the heel of the foot, designed for kicking in doors. This kick hit hard, knocking all the air out of me and sending me to the ground, gasping. He immediately came over to me, concerned. He showed me how to recover from being winded then wanted me to sit out the rest of the rounds. However, that wasn't going to happen and I got back in there. I got so used to being kicked like that in the stomach that if someone winded me, by the time they came over I was already up and ready to fight again. This tenacity would serve me well through life and would be needed. One Thursday, fight night was underway as usual, but I had no idea how much my tenacity was going to be tested. I was paired with a muscular man in his early twenties, a drywaller by trade that was two belts higher than I was. He also had much more experience in karate than the two belts could even represent. I was only fifteen or sixteen at this time, and my opponent seemed a lot older and more developed than I was. That evening we had a huge turnout, so there weren't enough footpads or headgear to go around. Both of us were without headgear, since we were more experienced than the other students in attendance that night. In addition, because he was a higher rank and had better control, the man was allowed to go without footgear. I ducked his jab punch and caught a full force wing kick. This is a cross between a roundhouse kick and a front kick and comes in a straight line at 45 degrees. His bare foot connected right to my temple, putting me in a daze that I'd often refer to as being standing KO'd. He was immediately concerned, as were the instructor and the other adults. The kick was so loud that all the others had stopped and come to offer me their assistance. The instructor didn't want a scene and instructed everyone else to return to their training. He came over to me, suggesting I sit down and take a break, but I refused because I was fine. I went right back into sparring, although I was pretty dazed and don't remember what happened during the rest of that evening.

Now, remember that although I was tenacious in sparring, I was also equally tenacious about not using these techniques outside of class, except as self-defence. However, one thing I was learning was self-confidence, which I ended up using in every aspect of my life. In the first year of starting Kempo Karate, I'd taken my school grades from failing three classes to achieving all As and Bs.

I still didn't know exactly where I fit in high school, but I did begin to branch out and talk to some different people in my classes other than just my core group of friends. Not only did Kempo Karate affect my school life, I found I also felt a lot better about myself. I was more confident and became more willing to try more things. By my second year of Kempo Karate, I moved on from having a paper route to having an actual job as a dishwasher in a Greek restaurant. Little did I know that my dream was about to be unexpectedly put on hold. One day at work, I was taking the garbage out to the dumpster and saw an RCMP officer. I was so excited. I wanted to be a police officer so badly and this was my opportunity to find out how. I just knew I had to talk to him. I told him that I was going to be a police officer when I grew up, I was getting good marks in school, and doing karate training. I was going to be the perfect officer. He asked how I was doing in French and I told him that even though I was doing well in school, that was one class I'd chosen not to continue with, since it would soon no longer be mandatory. I was getting made fun of a lot in this class and although I liked the work, I much preferred not to be ridiculed. He then informed me that I couldn't be a police officer with the RCMP, as the RCMP only hired people who were bilingual. I knew that French class just wasn't for me and chose not to take it as an elective after grade nine. I was already behind a year, so if I enrolled in French for the upcoming year I'd be in a class that was two grades below my own. French was also one of the classes I hadn't passed and it was embarrassing enough in some classes with kids a year younger. I wasn't at the point in life where I'd developed enough confidence to be in a class with people two years younger than me. As a result, I let the dream die that day.

Even though I'd given up the dream of becoming a police officer, because the only police organization I'd ever seen, or ever knew existed in Canada until I was in college, was the RCMP. I knew I couldn't get hired because I wasn't bilingual, but still watched all the cop shows and investigative shows I could find, maintaining my interest in observing others do that kind of job. However, I took that officer's word as a final authority that I couldn't be a police officer if I wasn't bilingual. I didn't like the idea that all the skills I could offer were all going to be overlooked because of one class in school. However, even though I didn't like it, I accepted it. I started to think of other options and knew the only other thing I was that passionate about was martial arts. Ever since I'd started in Kempo Karate, and experienced the difference it made in my life, I wanted to teach martial arts and run a club. I wanted to be in business for myself and make a difference in other young people's lives. However, I was concerned as I didn't see how that could be a full-time job. People weren't teaching at clubs full-time at that point. Everyone that was teaching, or at least everyone I'd heard of, taught martial arts as a side job. My first instructor owned a drywalling business, while my second instructor was a full-time mechanic. There was no rush in my mind though. After all, I was still in high school and graduating seemed miles away. I hadn't quite figured out what I'd do as a career but was very sure I couldn't be a police officer.

Lessons learned:
Bullying to.....
Maritial arts...
Dreams + goals....
Our destine begins in childhood with ....

Three Questions:
What was your childhood passion?
What or who supported it?
What was your biggest disappointment + how did you handle it?

Chapter Two - Time to Grow Up

As I was entering into my last two years of high school, it turned out that another move was in store for my family. As we began to plan a move, this time to Castlegar, BC, I was very sad to be leaving my Kempo Karate but excited about a new town, hoping that I'd find another karate club. My mom had gone to Castlegar and found the apartment where we'd be living, but my brothers and I hadn't yet seen the new place. One night I went to sleep after doing a relaxing meditation that I'd learned through Kempo Karate. It was almost as much hypnosis as it was meditation and I had a very vivid dream. I saw Castlegar, a place I'd never been before, and saw myself in our house. I described it as brown with a giant shrub outside. I knew I was high up, maybe on the second floor looking down, and I saw this girl. She was my age had long brown hair, beautiful blue eyes, the one aspect of my dream that I remembered the most vividly. In the dream the girl was moving some furniture. I knew I had to help her in, so I went downstairs. When I woke up, I told my mom that

I'd seen the house we were moving into in Castlegar. My mom was naturally sceptical and asked me to describe it. I explained that it was brown and I'd seen my window up high, as if my bedroom was on the top floor, and that there was a giant shrub in the yard. She was a little shocked but confirmed that the colour was correct and that we would be in an apartment on the second floor. It turned out that the shrub was true as well. When we did move to Castlegar I was very surprised when I realized how accurate my house description had been. Right beside the apartment was a path through some trees and shrubs, which was different to the picture I'd seen, but the idea was the same.

    After the dream, and once I'd described the apartment that we'd be moving to, I told my mom, that I'd seen the girl I was going to marry and described the girl in my dream. My mother was only slightly shocked because from the time I was young it wasn't uncommon for me to have these types of dreams. At the age of four, I'd fought with her and my dad to remove my training wheels because I'd a dream that I could ride my bike. They didn't want to because just the day before I'd been unable to ride without using the training wheels. However, after enough arguing, they decided to take off the training wheels and let me fall and learn my lesson. To their surprise, I took off riding without the help of the training wheels, just like I'd told them I could. Consequently, my mom remembered the conversations about the girl long after I did. I may have forgotten the conversation as soon as we'd had it.

We'd moved in the summer and my mom didn't want us to spend the warmer months without friends so, she signed us up as volunteers for the summer games that were going on in the area. I'm not an expert in all things, but whoever decided to use a teenager that [who] was brand new to the area as a guide, to help out-of-town bus drivers find unfamiliar locations, must have had some sense of humour. However, I did get to meet some very nice, patient, and understanding bus drivers and together we were able to find every place we needed to go. I do suspect whatever bus I was helping was always the last one to arrive. After all, I had no more information about the area, which areas of town they needed to go, or how to get to any of the locations. My willingness to guide buses in unfamiliar towns would be a testament to my increasing confidence. After all, high self-confidence is being able to take on new challenges knowing that your skill will help you prevail. [about]

My mom and brother had jobs at the local high school. My mom registered people and did paperwork for the athletes and coaches. My younger brother made lunches for the athletes. My mom ended up working with Jeremy, who was a local teacher at the high school and also a member of the local karate club. This was once again a non-profit club, charging only $25 a month. They were doing a different style of karate than the Kempo in which I'd trained. It was a style called Shotokan, but I was back in martial arts. When my mom came home with this news, I had no idea how much it was going to change my life. At the time I was simply excited to continue my love of martial arts and karate. I was excited that the instructor lived nearby and was able to give me a ride on karate nights, as we still didn't have a car. What I didn't know, and would take me years to learn, is just how much my karate instructor, Maurice, would help define my life. Not only would he teach me karate, he would also teach me about life. He'd take me on road trips, push me to attend college, and teach me to never accept defeat, never be afraid to do something new, because if someone else could do it, so could I. But I'm getting ahead of myself, as this was just going to be the first class, at which I had a great time. This style of karate was different than the one I was used to, but there were also a lot of similarities. The kicks were the same, although they did fewer variations than I'd already known. The punches of Shotokan used a very traditional format, one I'd only seen in a karate book up to that point, but it was a great club and I was having fun. That night I was introduced to another teenager about my age called Lyle and we instantly became fast friends. I also met another young man called Yuvraj. We'd also become friends, but not to the level of Lyle and me. Twenty-one years later Lyle and I would still be best of friends, and his friendship was going to come in very handy.

Things were going well and I was having a wonderful summer. One day I was sitting in my room, just relaxing with nothing really on the go. I was just enjoying the cool breeze from my window when I heard some noise outside. I went over to the window to see what was happening and it appeared that the people from the apartment below us were moving out. I then saw a girl with long brown hair. When she looked up, I remembered those beautiful blue eyes from the dream I had before we moved to Castlegar. I ran out of my room, excitedly telling my mom, I suspect very loudly, that I'd just seen the girl of my dreams, the girl I was going to marry. My mom encouraged me to go down and ask if they could use some help moving. So I went down as fast as I could be and helped the girl's family. She introduced herself as Trina and her mom told me she was Miss Castlegar. My first thought was that this was an exaggeration and her mom merely meant she knew everybody in Castlegar. The second thought I had was astonishment that I'd found a beauty queen. I was instantly taken back to my days in Creston, where Mrs. Creston had lived right by my place. Me and my friend Joey, whom I'd met when I first moved to Creston, made many bike trips back and forth down the street right by my house. After talking for a while, Trina realized I was new to the community and gave me her phone number so we could go on bike rides and I'd have someone to have fun with. We did hang out and go on some bike rides.

then I asked her out, asking her to be my girlfriend. However, she said no in a rather unkind fashion, so we continued being friends. I tried to impress her by jumping off high things and even breaking rocks. That's right, even breaking rocks, a skill that I'd learned through Kempo Karate. Yet Trina remained unimpressed and as school started in the fall, we became causal acquaintances at best. I was making friends, was busy with karate, and had my trusty sidekick, my younger brother, Justin. I had a different experience at this high school. Right from the first day people knew me as the karate guy, so I didn't get picked on at all. In fact, it seemed as if there was a lot less of that kind of thing altogether at the school. I was enjoying karate, learning a lot from Maurice. At the time Maurice's kids were already all grown up and had moved out, but I also felt like he treated me just like one of his kids. My friends Yuvraj and Lyle were into weightlifting, so I decided I should get a membership and start working out too. I was making a lot more money by then too, as I had a part-time job at McDonald's. I began to develop a lot more confidence with weightlifting, karate skills, and Maurice's encouragement. Maurice would drive Lyle and I to tournaments and I was able to increase my confidence, as I became successful at winning medals.

    In grade twelve, my Uncle Larry gave us his old computer and this was my first experience with a personal computer. My only prior experience had been at a typing course in school, but I'd never had a computer in my own house or had time to use one, other than during a couple of school classes. My confidence had increased quite a bit, so I asked to design a website for the karate club, despite the fact I'd never seen a code or heard of HyperText Markup Language (HTML). Building the website was a great experience, a wonderful lesson in just doing something you want to, without limitation. I just knuckled down and taught myself how to use HTML and build an awesome website, with the full support from Maurice. After building the site I was even more interested in computers so I took a couple more computer courses in school, discovering that I had a very natural knack for computers and coding. Sometimes my gift would be a curse for my classmates. On one occasion, our class went from having a whole period to work on a project to just five minutes. I figured out a faster way by simply having the confidence to try something that I thought might work, even though the textbook didn't mention the technique. I was done after only about five minutes of the first class. I then showed my friend how to do what I did and she was done too. We returned to class the next day and when the teacher asked who was finished, only she and I put up our hands. The teacher gave the other students the remainder of the time in the class to work on it. He was then intrigued enough to ask how I was done already. I showed him the technique I'd used and the class was then given five minutes to complete it.

Computer and coding classes weren't the only classes I loved. I liked many others as well, but still had no idea what I was going to do with my life. Things were also moving much faster than I'd ever anticipated. High school was ending, so I was going to have to grow up and make a decision. I just didn't know what to do, so I decided that since I already had a job at McDonald's and was making some money, I might as well just work for a year while I decided what to do. I knew I was very good with computers, but I was also phenomenal at law, scoring just about 100 percent on every test. Without ever studying for a single moment, law just made sense and seemed to naturally resonate with me. All I had to do was show up in class, listen to the teacher, and I retained all the knowledge we were taught that day. Not only that, I was still able to recall it years down the road. Law came so naturally to me. I thought maybe I can do something with law, but I didn't want to be a lawyer. I didn't feel that would work with my nature and personality. At that time, I still believed that becoming a police officer wasn't an option because I wasn't bilingual. I was completely unaware of how many other policing options existed, that maybe didn't require an officer to be bilingual.

Maurice and other adult members of the karate club encouraged me to go to college, to get a higher education and make something of myself. My mother had never really pushed the issue either way, although she did believe it would be a good idea to apply for scholarships. So, I respectfully followed their advice and started applying for all the scholarships I saw, and ended up being awarded $1,100 in scholarships and bursaries. I decided I'd apply at the local college in a program called Computer Information Systems, or CIS for short. I already had a love of computers, I was naturally good at using them, and the local college had a program. So now my future was set. I'd become a computer programmer. When college started, I must say I still didn't know if I was making the right choice. On my first day, it turned out I needed to upgrade some other courses before I could be enrolled in the CIS program. For example, I'd have to do a year of general studies. College was a lot of fun, but a lot more informal than I'd suspected or had been used to. Teachers didn't seem to care whether or not I showed up to class, whether I paid attention, or just sat there. Life at the dorm was awesome. I had a pool table just steps from my room, lots of friends, and a nice big gym in which to work out. This would ultimately lead to one of the biggest learning lessons of my life.

As I was enjoying working out and not attending class, I decided maybe I should become a professional bodybuilder and make my money doing that. However, I was pretty scrawny, weighing only 155 pounds and six feet tall, and the products I was using weren't allowing me to increase my size that much. I decided that I needed to find something else, something to help me get bigger and bigger. I found someone who was selling steroids and started using them. Almost instantly, I noticed an increase in my energy and I was putting on muscle fast. I started to become obsessed about how my muscles looked and how much weight I could do in the gym. I became hyper-focused on that and, as a result, many other areas of my life were going way off the rails. I'd opted out of my first kyu test, the last test before black belt, so that I could train more karate, but as soon as the muscle started packing on, I just stopped going to karate altogether. School went downhill very fast as well. I started spending more than four hours a day in the gym, with probably an additional two hours looking at myself in various mirrors. The rest of my day entailed eating, more than I ever had before, followed by copious amounts of sleep, which I seemed to require. When the first semester of college had finished, I was kicked out and asked not to enrol in the second semester. However, I found out that I could have a meeting with the college and maybe get back in. I had the meeting and used my extremely silver tongue to explain how I'd changed, learned from my past failure, and made adjustments to be the best student the college had ever seen. However, the second semester was somehow worse than the first. I barely ever went to classes and was losing friends faster than I could make them. I was getting bigger and achieving feats of strength that I'd never imagined possible, but that was all that was going for me. I was also out of control emotionally. I constantly felt cloudy mentally, in a way I'd never previously experienced. I became unreliable as my life consisted of eating, sleeping, or working out. College ended and it was time to go back home with my tail tucked between my legs. After all those years after grade ten, where I'd achieved some of my greatest success, I was now going home after a massive failure. It seemed that the expectations of friends and family regarding me being college-educated had vanished. And to top it off, I was so mentally foggy that I couldn't even formulate a plan for moving forward.

Lessons Learned:
One person can elevate a life

3 Questions
Who in your childhood or youth was your one person?

Chapter Three - Still Haven't Grown Up

The chapter title says it all. I'd grown big in terms of my muscles, but I hadn't grown up. I was out of college, too embarrassed to even attempt to go back if they'd begged me, but of course, they didn't. I still had no idea what I wanted to do. The only way I was going to figure it out was to go live my life. I was hired at Canadian Tire and was still going to the gym and working out, still using steroids occasionally. I'd use injectable or oral steroids. I wasn't using the same amount or as consistently as I did when I was in college, but I was using nonetheless. I found that working out was challenging without having the extra energy that steroids provided. I was out to experience life, and figure out where I wanted to go, and that was exactly what I did. I worked several different jobs during this time at Canadian Tire, with the carpenters union as a labourer, at CleanScene doing carpet cleaning and restoration, and at Safety Net Security. The Canadian Tire job was a lot of fun, or at least I had a lot of fun when I was there. I knew it wasn't my lifetime job, but there was a lot to learn and I always enjoyed the people I served, well most of them. I met a manager called Ron, who was an excellent person. He cared personally about the employees he managed and was always a patient teacher with employees, becoming a friend. One weekend we went on a road trip together with a couple of other guys from work. We traveled to visit Ron's relatives in Calgary and watched the Calgary Flames play live. This was such a huge experience for me, since I'd never watched a professional sports team play. I'd enjoyed and never missed a game with the Thunder, our Junior A team in Creston, but never seen anything at the level of NHL and it was beyond anything I'd ever imagined.

When I was in Calgary, I also met a childhood friend for coffee. He was working in Information Technology (IT) and talked about how much he had to work to make the job fun. In fact, he once dared all the guys that he could fix the problem with his eyes closed and sure enough, to the surprise of the other team members, he fixed the problem completely with his eyes closed. After talking to him, I felt that IT was just not going to be the job for me. I wanted excitement and more challenges than it sounded like he had. I certainly wasn't judging, as it sounded as if he'd found his career, not just a job like I had. At Canadian Tire, I worked inside the store in the sports department in the winter then outside in the garden centre in the summer months. It was in the summer that I ended up having a couple of life-changing events that still stick with me today. I met a manager called Ken, who was the manager of the garden centre and the housewares section. We became firm friends, not just at work but outside of work as well. I helped him do renovations on two houses that he owned and we'd have some really fun days working on projects. Ken was never someone who just took advantage of his friends. He always wanted to give back equally to what he'd received. Since I didn't have a house that he could help me work on, he offered to teach me to drive. He could have started me off slowly, driving in town, getting my feet wet a bit, but instead Ken decided the best time was when he needed to go to Trail, located about twenty minutes away from Castlegar on the highway. To this day, I don't know how he remained so calm in the passenger seat the first time I drove on a highway. I was fairly panicked and couldn't believe I was driving at 90 km/hr. It seemed like everything was coming at me so fast. Ken did remain very calm and spent several hours teaching me how to drive. Ken's calmness helped me learn to drive and overcome that brand new challenge. During this time I also met a supervisor in the warehouse at Canadian Tire who was selling his old grey 1988 four-cylinder Mustang for $300. He'd just bought a brand new car, didn't need or have room for two vehicles, and was good friends with Ken, so he gave me an awesome deal. I bought the car and used it to get my driver's license. This truly was such a feeling of accomplishment, being the first person in my family to own a vehicle. I was already in my twenties, had never driven before, or had access to a car whenever I wanted.

Having a car and a driver's license opened up a whole new world. I was able to go to the Carpenters Union hall and apply to be labourer, hoping to get a couple of day jobs on my time off to help add to my Canadian Tire income. The union paid much higher so I thought I'd only need a couple of days to make a big difference. One day, I got a call from the union. I was excited, as I'd only recently applied. It was short notice and I had to be there the next day. The job wasn't just for a couple days though. They said it was going to be a long job on a large project. I called Ron at Canadian Tire and told him I wouldn't be in the next day and that I'd quit. After a brief silence, he said okay. Our friendship would never be the same after that. I don't know if he took it personally, but I was simply chasing the money and opportunity. I didn't stop to think about the friendship I was damaging or the bad practice of quitting without giving any notice. I went and worked for the carpenters union, which was completely different to what I'd experienced in any other job. I was thrown off by the idea of pacing work and not just going all out. I'd always had the mindset that you did everything as fast as you could and then move on to the next task. However, on some days I was told not to work so hard. The boss even told me that he didn't want to see me work that hard again. One day I was asked to collect all the pieces of metal used for the forms and place them in a bucket. I filled the bucket then checked the weight. It was still good and I could carry it, so I put more and more in. I filled the buckets as much as possible, so that I'd have to make fewer trips and use fewer buckets. I completed the job, went on to my next task, but was then approached by one of the journeyman carpenters. He asked me not to load things so heavily and carry them because they exceeded WCB carrying limits. He also informed me that he and the other carpenter had to empty the buckets and split them up because they couldn't carry them. The other big surprise I learned from working with the union was about job descriptions. I was used to everyone helping out to win as a team, not as familiar with defined roles that one didn't step outside of. However, with the union even if there was a safety risk, such as a nail sticking out of a board, I wasn't allowed to fix it with a hammer. I simply wasn't permitted to do something outside my job description.

I enjoyed the job and it was outside, which I always enjoyed, and the pay was more money than I'd ever made up to that point in my life. However, winter was approaching and I was laid off, just waiting on the job board to go out to work. I was off for about a year and never did get called back. The year was very slow for work and even though I was fairly high on the board, there were no calls. I was okay waiting for the year with the possibility of going back. I was making more money being laid off than I'd made at Canadian Tire. After about a year, I was getting bored. I could only spend so many nights playing video games. I was also starting to wonder if I was ever going back to work, so I started to get anxious. I ended going back to Canadian Tire, doing the same job I'd done before. I continued to work there until I heard about a job at Clean-Scene. It involved carpet cleaning and restoration, two things I knew absolutely nothing about, but the pay was a lot better than my current job. I applied for the job and had an interview with the owner. We immediately established an instant rapport and both knew that I'd be an excellent fit for the company. I started working for them, after giving proper notice to Canadian Tire, which felt like growth since I felt a lot better knowing I didn't just up and leave again. At Clean-Scene I started in the carpet cleaning section. I was always eager to attend courses and was so proud on the day I became a carpet cleaning technician. I enjoyed the people I worked with and I can't remember a day, even when crawling though sewage soaked insulation, that I didn't have a lot of fun and truly enjoy every moment I was at work. I always loved the disaster clean up and restoration side of the business. Even then, I was drawn to the feeling of being the person someone relied on when they needed help, calling them in their moment of need.

I was still living at home with my mother, which was creating a lot of tension. I'd been living on my own in dorms for eight months. I loved that taste of independence, with no one telling me what to do, or how or when to do it. That feeling of freedom drove me to rent an apartment of my own from Maurice and my younger brother, Justin, moved in. I was working at Clean-Scene and enjoying the job. I was also still occasionally using steroids and working out at the gym. One day, I was getting ready for a workout and needed to inject myself with steroids, but I was rushed and not very careful. I'd been warned that I should never get the steroids in a vein. I wasn't sure whether I'd hit a vein, or if I'd put the steroids only in the muscle. That evening I ended up having to go to the hospital, suffering from some debilitating pain in my stomach. The doctors never could figure it out, but I often wondered if the pain had been caused by steroids in the vein. I became cautious about using steroids any longer and a follow-up doctor's appointment would seal the deal and close that chapter. I'd gone to the doctor because I was having some weird chest pain. The doctor asked if I was using steroids, because young men my age didn't normally develop breasts, which was what was happening to me. I didn't need to wait for a third event to happen, as those first two scared me more than enough. I decided that if I was going to quit using steroids, I was going to go beyond just quitting temporarily and knew that I needed to quit for good. When I did, I had steroids in the house that I could access at any point. I'm proud to say that I never touched steroids again after that moment.

But major changes in my life were just about to start and I had no idea how big those changes were going to be. One day after work, at the end of September 2001, my brother, Justin, had finished work and wanted to go to Tim Hortons for a bowl of chilli. Occasionally, we'd go and get some chilli and a doughnut, so I was quite happy to go. There was no way to anticipate what I'd end up getting that night. When we arrived at Tim Hortons, the girl working at the counter and taking our order was Trina. She'd moved away after high school and was now back. She said that she remembered that we used to have fun hanging out and wondered if I'd want to do something with her. I said of course and asked her if her number was still the same. She was impressed that I still remembered her phone number after all those years. Needless to say, I was so excited to do something with Trina. However, I'd read somewhere that I shouldn't call for at least twenty-four hours in case I appeared too eager, possibly even desperate. I kept myself busy with any task I could think of, everything I could do for twenty-four hours, to make sure I didn't call too soon, since I certainly didn't want to appear desperate. I finally did call and we decided that we'd go for a nice long walk. We quickly rekindled our friendship, but now both of us had matured and we had a different type of relationship than we'd had before. Our first outing quickly led to another, then another, before we were falling very much in love. We continued to date, many times choosing to have nice long walks on which we just walked and talked, go sit by the river, and just talk and laugh. Finally, on one of our walks, we were sitting on a bench by the river, looking out over the water, talking about everything including our dreams and where our lives were going. As we sat there talking, Trina looked at me.

"So what's going on with us?" she asked.

I knew what she was asking, but was being very cautious because of the several dating rejections I'd already received from Trina.

"Are you're asking if we're dating?" I replied. "I'd like to yes, but I wasn't going to ask again."

Believe it or not, this somewhat unique conversation began our official dating relationship. Although we'd just started dating, it would have been hard to anticipate that our lives were about to change in ways that we weren't yet aware of and would expand beyond anything either of us had imagined up to that point. While we were on one of our walks, I told Trina that I'd been talking to a friend who'd gone to Lethbridge College and had received a diploma in a programme called criminal justice, related to policing. I felt this was the right program for me to take and explained that I'd put in an application. Not only that, I'd been accepted into the programme and would be going to the college in

September.

Trina was concerned that I'd be leaving for Lethbridge and wondered what was going to happen with us. Were we going to try dating long distance? If so, how were we going to make it work? She told me that she wasn't going to be moving in with me in Lethbridge if we were dating and that she didn't intend to live with someone to whom she wasn't married. By this time, we'd only been dating for a couple of months, but as I mentioned we were truly falling in love. One day Trina said that she loved me more than I could ever love her. I told her this wasn't true and that I loved her much more. She stated that I didn't know how much she loved me, at which point I believe I threw out a sarcastic, joking comment about marriage. Trina didn't flinch and in fact seemed quite excited about the idea, although I should point out that this hadn't been intended as a proposal. However, her excitement seemed to solve a few problems. If I did propose to her and we were married, we could both go to Lethbridge and live together while I was in college. So I set in motion a plan to propose to Trina, even though we'd only been dating for about three months. I'd already tested the waters with my joking comment, so I felt that there was a pretty good chance that she'd say yes. On our dates we started going over to my mom's house before we went for our walk. Trina always wanted to check her e-mail on my mom's computer, so I started the routine of having her check my e-mail every time as well. I always made sure that she waited for the home page to load up, mostly because my mom's computer was slow and needed to complete one task before it began a new one. To be honest, that wasn't very true. I was creating a webpage for my proposal and needed to have Trina in the habit of waiting for the home page to load up. Then one day in December 2001 Trina and I were on one of our regular dates, stopping at my mom's to check e-mails. Trina always remembered that she needed to wait for the home page to load. When it finally did, the words 'Trina I love you, so will you marry me?' were displayed on the screen. In the background, a character popped up his head and wiggled his eyes. When she turned around Trina noticed I was on my knees, with a ring waiting for her. Trina said yes and then we began the long, arduous wedding planning stage, although I'm pretty sure my actual part of planning was simply to show up on the appointed day. By May 2002, Trina and I were married and living together. We were all set to move to Lethbridge in August, in order to arrive there just before school started. Trina had found a job at a local Tim Hortons as an assistant manager and I was enrolled in college.

Chapter Four - A Dream Life

Trina and I had moved to Lethbridge and I was starting college. There was a lot of excitement going on in my life at that time. I'd just recently married my dream girl. I was starting college, completing my dream of being educated, and I was going to be the first person in my family to get a college diploma. I was also about to look at accomplishing another dream, one that had been pushed aside for many years. That was my dream of becoming a police officer and I hoped that the college program would teach me how that might be possible. Marriage to Trina was truly just what I'd expected, a total and complete dream. We had great times together and always made sure to make time for a lot of fun for the two of us. Lethbridge was a great community and provided many opportunities for young couples and college students to have a great time on a college budget. With several restaurants close by, we ate out fairly regularly, enjoying nice long dinners, with an appetizer, main course, and dessert, which allowed us to sit and talk. We'd chat about everything, including what I was learning in school, what she was doing at work, and what our future held. I always liked to tell Trina about unique things that I'd learned at college, many of which came from my English class. My English teacher was great and English was an exciting class. She had a way of bringing the class alive and presenting the information in a manner that was unorthodox, to say the least, I'm not even sure some of it would be appropriate for this book, although for a class of college kids, it was perfect. At one of our dinners, I asked Trina if she knew what the definition of pregnant was. She replied that the obvious explanation was related to having a child growing in her tummy. I then told her that the definition was 'someone who is highly significant'. We laughed at that definition, one that stuck in our minds, even to this day.

Trina and I continued many of the regular activities that we'd enjoyed when we were dating, which included nice scenic walks and watching many movies. We were spending lots of time together, really getting to know each other, and were also learning some great things about marriage, most importantly about communication. As I've said, many of our activities involved a great deal of talking, but not the type of communication that truly made a marriage work. We spend our time talking about what we were doing, what we were pursuing, and sharing stories about our past. We didn't focus on having deep conversations and delving into our likes and dislikes. Most weekends we'd take turns cooking breakfast for one another.

One of our most regular and favourite choices was toast, bacon, and eggs. I don't remember how this next story began, whether it was me or Trina that made the first breakfast, so for purposes of sharing this story I'll start with me doing it. One day, I made the breakfast eggs over easy and the bacon not crispy, but when it came time to make toast, I knew I liked mine very lightly toasted, some would say not toasted at all. I took a lot of flack over the years for making toast that way, being asked why I didn't just eat the bread raw, because it pretty much was. I loved to have the bread toasted just enough to melt the butter but was quite aware it wasn't a normal way of making or eating toast. So, wanting to make my wife's breakfast perfectly, I let her toast darken a bit more than mine, so that it was what I felt was regular toast. She ate her breakfast and thanked me for making it, with not a single complaint. I'd nailed it, right out of the gate, just as I'd intended. The following weekend, Trina cooked the breakfast, made the eggs over easy, the bacon not crisp and then made my toast, but it was much darker than I liked to eat it or had really ever had before. We went back and forth for months taking turns making breakfast. Every time I cooked the toast, mine was lightly toasted and hers was dark. Every time Trina made breakfast, she made hers lightly toasted and mine quite dark. We never paid attention to how the other was making their breakfast, until one day I did finally notice.

"Why is it when you make breakfast, you always make your toast perfect, just lightly toasted, and then you make mine dark?" I asked.

"Well, I thought you liked your toast dark," she replied. "You always make mine dark, so I thought that was because you liked it that way."

We both spent months making the other person's toast dark, believing that because they made ours dark that must be how they preferred to eat theirs. This was one of our greatest lessons in the importance of communication in marriage, although in this specific case darker toast didn't really mean anything to either of us. It was the principle about open, honest communication that was the real gem, about letting your partner know what you like and what you don't like. Making sure not to make assumptions and just gently discussing the issues. This was most certainly a year of dreams, even though there were some marriage hiccups. We were stumbling our way through, but it was so meaningful to be sharing life with my dream girl and to be starting our first set of combined dreams.

The first one of these featured my intertwined goals of getting a college diploma and hopefully learning how to become a police officer. Getting a college diploma was going to be a huge dream for me, a chance to redeem myself following my early attempt at college when steroids took over my life. I had an opportunity to remind myself and inspire others that everyone falls at some point and that's not important. It's what they do with that and I'd got back up, dusted myself off, and tried again. College was also an opportunity to be the first, such as the first person in my family to gain a college diploma. Being the first to do things and being a leader always fit my personality perfectly. I loved to be confident enough to lead the way, not feeling that I had to wait for someone else to make a path for me or show me how to accomplish the goal. College was also going to help me decide if policing was truly a career for me. Maybe, just maybe, there was a way of getting a policing job with the RCMP without having to be bilingual. I can't say enough good things about Lethbridge College, and more specifically their criminal justice policing program. This was designed by educated police officers. Most of my instructors were also former police officers and knew what it was like to do the job. Even the program head had been a police officer in the military until he retired. That was one man who commanded a ton of respect whenever he entered a room.

Part of the program was also designed to make the criminal justice students stand out from all the other students in the college, requiring all the students to dress in business attire on Fridays, the males were in suits and ties, the female students also in business attire, sometimes in suits as well. The explanation for this was to get the students, and the potential police officer, to be used to standing out in a crowd, to be accustomed to having people look or sometimes even stare at them. For me, none of that stuff mattered. It was more just an opportunity to wear a smart suit, since I always liked to dress nicely. I probably could have worn a suit every day. The criminal justice program was also designed to help people make decisions regarding their lives and future careers. The first year of the program was designed so that students had general courses that applied to several jobs, with courses like English, law, and alternative dispute resolution. There were three branches of the program that students could enter after the first year. Students could go into criminal justice corrections, criminal justice policing, or over to fish and wildlife game warden enforcement. One thing that became very apparent in the first year was how much I still loved law classes and excelled in them. I didn't have to put in countless hours of study learning law and just seemed to understand it. As long as I paid attention in class, I always retained the information and once again quite often scored in the top of the class, a feeling I was used ever since I'd started karate back in high school. I enjoyed all my other classes and found that everything seemed to be a fit for me. I struggled more in English than any other class. I just didn't have the same level of interest that I had in my other courses. Martial arts were also still a big part of my life and I began teaching a self defense class at the college. The class was a combination of the several martial arts I'd studied. I'd show some different hold escapes and locks that I'd learned in

Kempo Karate, my favourite locks, as well as the what I believed to be the most relevant techniques for future police officers. I felt like I was beginning to find my way in life, but I still wasn't sure whether policing or my natural ability with the law should dictate my career. As law class went on, and we did some scenarios, the same thing was true in college law that had been true from high school. I was a great lawyer and could use language very well. I was skilled at finding little loopholes to get people off in our mock trials. I think this was due to my nature of always wanting to see a problem from as many points of view as possible. I'm sure I could argue for days with myself on just about any topic, if I so desired. However, I did decide that, morally at least, being a lawyer wasn't going to be the correct path for me. I believed in justice and fairness. I believed that everyone has the right to be treated as innocent until proven guilty. I believed in rights that were guaranteed to all of us, so I did believe in the legal system. I simply didn't believe I could use language and loopholes to get a person acquitted, even if they'd committed a crime. I knew I'd happily battle for someone that had been falsely accused. Yet I knew that I'd have had a hard time living with myself if I obtained an acquittal for someone I knew was guilty or found out was guilty, as much as I believed strongly in the justice system. For me that included justice for victims of crime as well.

As my criminal justice program continued,

the dream of policing was revived. I realized that the reasons for my belief from years earlier, that it was futile to even try, had either changed or had never existed. The RCMP and several other police services were open to taking all good candidates, even those who weren't bilingual. I couldn't believe how close I was to my goal. I was enrolled in the program, being successful, and learned that the program could truly lead to my goal of becoming a police officer.

However, life is full of surprise and excitement, with many unexpected twists and turns. My life was about to take the most drastic turn I'd ever experienced up to that point. One day I got home from school and Trina hadn't yet arrived. She was very excited when she finally got home and wanted to go for dinner at our favourite restaurant. Over dinner, she looked as if she was going to burst she was so excited. I don't even know if we'd even received our drinks when she made her announcement.

"I'm highly significant," she said.

You may remember when I explained to Trina the definition of pregnant, so I instantly knew what she meant. That's right, Trina was pregnant and we were in for the most wonderful change of our lives. There was a lot to do at this time and of course this was our first child. Neither of us was familiar with what to do and we had all the same questions as other first-time parents. Are we going to do things right? Are we going to know what to do? How is our relationship going to be affected? We wondered if we'd be best to try to answer those questions ourselves while living eight hours away from our families. We decided that at the end of the first year of college, we'd move back to Castlegar to have our baby and be close to our families.

On June 20, Trina gave birth to a beautiful baby girl we named Cierra. I was back working at Clean-Scene, enjoying cleaning carpets, restorations, and providing for Trina and my little girl. I'd applied to the Calgary Police Service but didn't pass the panel interview stage. They were looking for someone with a little more life experience. I'd also applied to the RCMP, but in an attempt to be as honest as I could, I ended up exaggerating the number of times I'd used steroids. As a result, the RCMP deferred me for two years. At that point, the dream was alive and one of the rare times in my life, where I asked for and accepted help on how to accomplish my goal, what path I needed to take, but now I'd been shown that path and there was no chance of some minor setbacks dissolving my dream again. I did believe that education was going to be important to achieving that goal, so I decided I needed to go finish the second year of college and get my diploma. We decided that Trina should stay behind where my mom and also her parents lived, so that she could have family support with our beautiful baby. I went back to Lethbridge alone to continue my education and pursue my dream. Now it was more important than ever to be successful because I had a family to provide for. Trina and I made sure that we visited each other many times over the following eight months, whether it was her and Cierra coming to visit me or me going to visit them. During that school year, I started working with a security company. I became good friends with the owner and the manager of the company. I enjoyed the type of work and being at the company throughout the whole school year. When that came to a close, it was one of the proudest moments of my life. Trina and my daughter made the trip to Lethbridge to see my graduation and I'd completed that chapter of my life. I'd graduated with an overall B average and was now ready to pursue my goal of becoming a police officer. However, I was still in a deferral period, so I wanted to make sure I gained the correct kind of life experience to be successful.

I was now a college graduate, so I decided to accept a supervisor position within the security company and move my whole family to Brooks, Alberta. Trina began babysitting at our house so that she could stay home with Cierra and we could still make the income needed to live. After success as a supervisor, I was offered a manager position with the company, managing both the loss prevention and uniformed security guard operations at various contracted stores the company served in Medicine Hat. I was also designated as the company's private investigator for the area. When I accepted the job, I had no idea of the mess I was walking into. Most of my staff members were ready to quit and were undertrained and under-motivated. This was my first real taste of management and I loved it. I was a natural leader and because I was good at looking at problems from many different angles, I recognized the importance of speaking to the staff and looking at the issue from their point of view. I identified that the two things they needed were a feeling of being listened to and some training to help them feel more confident. I immediately implemented procedures for staff to be heard in regards to their work issues. I also provided training to the staff on using tactical communication, how to verbally gain compliance, and how to verbally respond in situations where people were yelling or resistant. As a result, I was able to keep all my staff, as well as motivate and train them. One day the owner of the company came by and I was talking to him about all the wonderful things I was doing.

"I'll believe that the procedures you've implemented are working when the number of arrests goes up," he said.

He also mentioned that in the entire history of the company, the Medicine Hat district had never beaten the Lethbridge district. I accepted the challenge and the steak dinner prize that was offered if I won. Well, that year I got my steak and it was just a little more delicious than any previous steak, as I felt I'd earned it. In defiance of the odds, I accomplished the task of having more arrests, by respecting the employees, listening to them, and providing the tools they needed. At our year-end party, my staff surprised me with presents. I was the only manager in the company to ever receive gifts from the staff. I'd reaffirmed at that point that I was a great manager and a great leader. I thought that maybe I should stay in security management. However, I started to see the writing on the wall regarding my future. I could see the stores were more interested in getting the best bargain for their buck. They were happy to have a minimal number of arrests or even no arrests of shoplifters at all, as long as they could get a better price. Their insurance premiums dropped the same amount either way, whether the security company they'd hired made an arrest, deterred shoplifters, or did neither of those things. I resigned from my position as manager and we once again moved back to BC. I wasn't sure If I was making a good decision, although I thought the company was going to lose a lot of contracts to a cheaper company that had come into the area. What if I was wrong? What if it was the best job for me after all? It turned out to be a great decision, even though it had been so hard to leave. Within a year the company had lost most of their contracts and ended up letting many of the staff go, closing down the Brooks and Medicine Hat district.

Back in BC, I continued with security work, working for a fairly large company in Trail, BC.

Trina had taken a job at the local hospital as a unit clerk and was making more money than I was. My mother lived about three or four blocks away so she was able to help take care of Cierra if we needed her. With both Trina and I doing shift work, we found it was pretty easy to usually have one of us at home. I worked for the company for about a year, but always felt like something was missing in my life. Some excitement simply wasn't there, nor was there a sense of fulfillment, and I was just going through the motions. However, there was very little, if anything, to investigate or have to diffuse. I mostly spent time driving around by myself, going to the locations of the buttons I had to hit to show I was doing patrols, as requested. I was excited when I became certified to be an operator of the company's second ambulance. I'd attended two calls for first-aid and felt the adrenaline of having to get somewhere quickly to assist someone in need. I also was able to experience how great it felt to be the person that showed up and helped someone. Even though the calls were very minor, I still enjoyed being the person someone turned to when they needed help. I knew this wasn't enough though, since there were very few calls. I loved the calls I was able to attend, but there wasn't enough excitement or enough helping for me. I knew I had to continue to pursue my dream of becoming a police officer and by then my deferral with the RCMP was over. I put in an application to the RCMP and again started the process, attempting to realize a lifelong dream.

During this time, Trina had become highly significant again and we were excited about the next addition to our family. It was a perfect time for me to get a career and be able to take care of our growing family. The RCMP process went a lot smoother that time. I took the time to prepare, to sit down and know exactly how many times I'd used the steroids. I also emphasized that when I chose to stop, I did so in the best manner I could, to make sure I'd never resort to using steroids again. I knew that by having the steroids readily available, and making the choice every day to not use them, meant that I'd quit for life. I was able to present all this new information, explaining where I'd exaggerated usage in the past by not being prepared. I also explained that the amount of usage I'd provided the first time I applied had been the amount I planned to use when I'd started using steroids, but in reality the length of time I'd actually used was much less than that. I verified the truthfulness of all these statements with a pre-employment polygraph and was hired with a date to go to the RCMP Academy, Depot Division, commonly known as Depot, in August 2007.

Chapter Five - When Dreams Become Reality

Going to Depot in Regina has to epitomize the meaning of the phrase 'with great sacrifice comes great reward'. On the one hand, I was given a realistic opportunity to achieve my dream, while on the other I was asked to sacrifice my family and paycheque for six months. I had to give up my salary, wasn't allowed to have a job on the side nor allowed to collect EI, so I had to figure out how to support a family for six months without receiving any money. This choice would have been a lot easier with a guarantee. However, that didn't exist. There were several situations where I could have gone to Depot, given up the money, and not ended up with my dream job as a police officer. Naturally, this was a gamble, but I'd gone so far already that I couldn't imagine not taking the gamble at that point in the game. I figured out a way to be able to go to Depot, support my pregnant, or highly significant, wife, along with my daughter, gambling on success for my dream job. Support was my biggest asset in that stage of my life. My wife was a strong partner that was able and willing to put in extra hours and extra work to help make my dream, and ultimately our dream, a reality.

The first day I arrived at Depot I was star struck and couldn't believe I was really there. I was truly on the home stretch to becoming a police officer. I arrived at Depot from the airport and received my instructions and room assignment. I'd wondered how I'd function in barrack-type sleeping and living arrangements, I'd never lived with anyone other than family and even then were never more than four of us in a house. I was relieved when I found out that although we'd all be together as a troop, we had separate rooms except for one other person. It seemed odd as a twenty-eight-year-old person to be sharing a bunk bed with another adult, but I liked the sound of that much better than sharing a room with thirty other adults. I arrived at my room and eventually met my roommate Steve. It was quite surprising that being placed together by the alphabetical order of our last names could pair such a like-minded duo. We'd become great friends throughout training and far beyond that time. Not all room pairings or the troop, in general, were as like-minded as I'd initially believed they would be. When I'd met the members of our big brother troop, they'd warn us of troop infighting, providing examples they'd experienced or observed while being at Depot. This was the troop that was further into their twenty-four weeks that was assigned to show us the way. They talked about people quitting Depot, or getting kicked out for undesirable behaviour. The members of our troop had quite an opinionated debate on the likelihood of anyone quitting. It was hard for me to fathom that someone would work that hard to get there, sacrifice that much, and then just quit. I was surprised at the number of opinions that were shared, the unique reasoning process that individuals had, and the ability of people to support their opinions. I firmly believed that no one would work that hard to quit and that if they left, it was because they were unsuitable. Others believed no one could get kicked out because the hiring process had too many steps and would eliminate everyone who was unethical. And with thorough background checks and polygraph examinations, there was a lot of validity to that argument. The third option was an injury, which was the one thing we all accepted as a potential reality. I was of the mindset that I wouldn't quit, not when I'd worked so hard, not when Trina and I had sacrificed to make a reality. They'd have to remove me because of a severe injury. I always had a strong sense of not quitting since I was young, but I was about to learn an extreme aspect of that personality trait.

One day a member of the troop, we'll call him John, challenged me.

"This martial arts choke is inescapable," he said. "Once it's on, nothing can be done to get out."

I laughed, knowing several escapes and counters very well, explaining to him that there were a number of ways out. John refused to accept that I was telling the truth and wanted to put me in the hold and show me. He wrapped his arms around my neck, locked it in then asked me to escape, which I did after only a few seconds, reversing the lock. However, I'd added some movement to the lock, making it tougher to escape. Expecting a tap, which was common in martial art grappling classes, I held the lock, presuming it wasn't effective, always listening and feeling for signs of danger, as we were training not trying to hurt one another. I realized he was on the verge of passing out, so I released.

"Why didn't you just tap?" I asked, puzzled. "I thought the hold wasn't on right until I heard you about to pass out."

His reply still haunts me to this day.

""Cops don't quit," he said.

I was quite upset with this response. I explained that you have to tap when training, otherwise your partner doesn't know if they're hurting you. I couldn't believe that he was willing to pass out or worse, simply to prove the point that he wouldn't quit. Luckily for him, this was a technique I'd trained often and very well through martial arts, always placing the emphasis on safely training. As a result, I knew which responses to be watching for that indicated someone might be in danger of passing out. Yet this level of not quitting seemed extreme to me. We all have physical limits that we can push too, ones that if we go beyond will cause injury. I always believed there was wisdom in finding that balance, recognizing that point and stepping back or just backing off completely. I was able to empathize with my troopmate though, as I'd also learned that lesson by pushing too far past those points, and as a result getting injured. I'd started to learn by the age of twenty-eight that there usually wasn't a pot of gold at the end of the rainbow and that finding and respecting my body's limit, and then working to exceed it slowly with education or training, was much smarter than getting injured and having to recover.

Depot was phenomenal for learning to develop realistic limitations and identify where you were actually limited and where you just quit out of lack of self-confidence. The first weekend was about the only true free weekend, a time where you had a chance to meet the troop you'd be taking the journey with. The very first challenge was to have confidence and work hard to do things that I'd never done before. I'd made a bed and kept a clean room of course, but never to the standards I'd be taught that Sunday before training began. I was suddenly expected to go from throwing my blankets on my bed in the morning at home to making a bed with perfectly square corners, the sheets and blankets all perfectly spaced how far they were folded down from the top of the bed and each other. Although this was one of the simplest limitations I'd push past, it was the same principle of being open-minded to accept a new routine, even if temporarily, as I was twenty-eight when I went to Depot and had already established several set routines in my life, ones that were now being retrained. I received my instructions on how to polish my boots, some of them requiring polishing formulas, how to hang my uniform, which direction, and even which buttons were done up. All these new rules felt overwhelming. I felt a level of uncertainty with this brand new way of living. Prior to Depot, I'd hang all my dress clothes but I never cared which of the buttons were done up and I'd certainly never previously polished anything I owned. This was where confidence really showed itself, the mindset of being able to know I'd be successful, even though I was doing something brand new. My ability to master this new task of room organization would be tested in a surprise inspection and two informal inspections. The surprise inspection was aptly named. I arrived to find my room tossed, which kind of reminded me of my bachelor days living with my brother. We were provided with a list of deficiencies that we had to make right and my room alone on this inspection would be more than the troop total in the next two inspections. I guess I hadn't mastered hanging up my gear or making my bed.

As the first formal inspection approached, I knew I had a lot of work to do. However, I was determined to be successful. I stayed up all night, checking, double-checking, and triple-checking buttons, and decided to not sleep so I wouldn't mess up the bed. I probably only had two hours sleep that night, but when the inspection results were announced and my room had passed, two things happened. Firstly, I felt huge relief to know how successful I was, despite the fact that just a few days earlier I'd failed the surprise inspection. Secondly, I now knew what the expectations were so could better focus my time to achieve still more success. When the final inspection came around, the majority of the troop was scrambling, doing the same thing they'd done before, staying up all night, while my roommate and I were eating pizza and heading to bed nice and early. As we began to head to bed, one of the troop members announced very loudly that no one had better fail the inspection the next day, while glaring at me and my pit partner, which is the Depot version of roommate. We just laughed and headed to bed, suspecting that we'd figured out what was required and knew that we could get up early and with focused intention have the same results as before. At the end of the day, the results were announced and two rooms had failed, but not my room. I'd been given a new task, fallen down (surprise inspection), got up and dusted myself off (first formal inspection), and excelled at learning how to better focus my efforts, spending a fraction of the time on the final inspection and still being successful.

The next challenge was physical fitness. Although I'd kept myself in what I considered decent shape, when I saw the required goals to be successful and pass Depot in order to get hired, I had some doubt, However, I knew they were going to have to drag me out kicking and screaming, because no matter what the pain level, I'd keep pushing forward. On the very first run, I thought I was going to have to quit and simply wasn't able to go any further. I refused to quit and continued to push, long after I thought my body should be physically tired, and made it. Yet this didn't fill me with hope, only with more concern. If that run was so hard and was nowhere near the distances or time I'd need to pass Depot, how was I going to make it through the longer runs? Success in this area was going to require a different strategy. Belief would not be enough. I needed to have unwavering determination to just run, run, and when I was in pain run some more. The more I began to push, I realized that much of my physical fitness was just a mindset. I hadn't learned where my body was actually exhausted, only where my mind thought it should be exhausted. I learned to push through pain, adapting my training to find success. Very early on I developed shin splints from all the running I was then doing. Shin splints weren't bad, although they were painful. However, they didn't put me in danger of going home and losing all the hard work I'd put in. Stress fractures were my biggest concern at that time. I'd heard of cadets being sent home after week ten, eleven, twelve, or even thirteen for stress fractures. The thought of being halfway through training and having to go home was hard to imagine and would have ended my dream. I took care where I could, but had to keep pushing past the pain to get the physical fitness needed to pass the benchmarks. Then my shins became so bad that the doctor told me that I needed to have a stress fracture test done. I knew very little about the test, other than the doctor would use a tuning fork to hit my shin. Apparently, the vibration was extremely painful and I gathered from people who had been sent home that they verbally indicated the problem to the doctor with a scream.

I'd sacrificed too much by that point, gone too far, and wasn't prepared to allow this issue to send me home. I thought back to when I was a teenager and learnt mind over matter when a wasp crawled up my pant legs to sting me six times. I just focused elsewhere until my eye started twitching and I knew I had to deal with whatever was causing the pain. I grabbed my pant leg with the wasp inside it and threw it in the toilet. I just couldn't go home, so I was determined to use that skill in the doctor's test. I went into his office, where he brought out the tuning fork, placed it on my shin then hit the fork. To my surprise and enjoyment, there was no pain to have to ignore. Luckily it was just severe shin splints and not a stress fracture. I had to take time off from running, but I found the stationary bike to be my best friend during that time, making sure I kept up my cardiovascular training. The three major benchmarks for running that I remember were the 1.5 mile, 3 mile, and 5 mile runs. I can't remember much about the runs other than I usually finished about mid-pack with the troop. I was successful in all three of the runs, finishing under the benchmarks required to move forward in Depot. Although this skill required tenacity and perseverance, as well as a belief I could and would, I utilized all of those to achieve success.

The third challenge was definitely the most serious of the three. The challenge was two-fold. Firstly, I had to leave my four-year-old daughter and pregnant wife behind in BC for six months. Secondly, I had to come together with thirty strangers and for the next six months develop and utilize them as my support system in order to be successful. Having a great pit partner was a start. Someone with whom I shared a lot of common ground made this a lot easier and I really ended up thinking of my pit partner, Steve, as a brother. I'd make a huge statement with my troop the first day we lined up together.

"Boy, this is the fattest troop I've ever seen," someone said, as we were lined up waiting for the dismissal at the end of the day.

I deduced from the tone that this person was joking and not meaning anything by it, so I responded.

"We're not a fat troop, sir. We're just built like polar bears and you wouldn't mess with a polar bear, would you?"

This saying had always meant something to me when I was working in security in Alberta. It was what my boss would always say if someone commented on my weight, telling them that I was built like a polar bear. However, when I said it that day, no one laughed.

"I don't know about that," said the person that had made the comment then walked away, as we were dismissed.

As we were walking into the building my troopmates bombarded me with questions, asking how I'd had the guts to say something like that first day to a corporal while I was just a cadet. I never responded to any of them, mainly because I didn't have an answer. I was always quick-witted like that, never minded back and forth teasing banter, and had always built strong relationships with my bosses in the past where I could say things like that to them. However, none of that mattered in this case, because I honestly thought it was another cadet that had made the comment. I had no clue it was corporal until troopmates asked me how I'd had the courage to make my remark. I had an 'oh no' moment when I found out it was a corporal and had an anxious couple of days, hoping I'd read the situation correctly and that the corporal hadn't left upset. Nothing ever came out of that interaction, so I guess I'd read it right. However, it made a huge statement of fearlessness to the rest of the troop and started that bonding process. I began to define my role as someone who'd speak up for the troop and protect my 'family'. I very quickly became an unofficial leader, a role that I look back on now as quite an honour. I hope that I did well by the people that followed my leadership or were inspired by my success or personality. I had two people come to me when they believed Depot wasn't right for them and were thinking about quitting. Even though this had baffled me at the start, I really listened to what they were feeling and tried to provide the best advice regarding what would be right for them and their families, not for me and my beliefs. After our conversations, both decided to leave and pursue another life. I don't believe I ever influenced their decisions. I just allowed myself to be a sounding board and active listener, so they could think out loud and draw their own conclusions.

I kept busy at Depot and by forming bonds with many great troopmates I have a lot of fond memories. I definitely class Depot as a great experience about which I have very few regrets. The one portion that I did regret was leaving my family. I was always the kind of person that preferred family to friends. My best friend growing up was my younger brother, Justin, and it was hard to find one of us without the other. When I got married, my best friend became my wife, Trina. When we had our first child, when I wasn't at work the only place I wanted to be was spending time with them. The only option I was left with during Depot was a phone call, but that was never as good as seeing them in person. Often there wasn't really enough time to call, with too many other things to be done. When I got the call that my wife had given birth to our son and that it had been a difficult birth, my heart broke that I wasn't there for her or for him. I'd taken time off from work for the birth of my daughter and allowed Trina to rest, letting my daughter sleep on my chest. I helped my wife through giving birth and could encourage her to do the things the doctor was asking her to do, while she ignored or snapped at him. The birth of my daughter was smooth and I was there the whole time. However, the birth of my son was a difficult one and I wasn't there for him or for Trina. I was eight weeks away from graduating, but that was the only real time I asked myself if the sacrifice was going to be worth it and wondered whether I'd made the right decision. In the end, I really felt as if I was making the correct sacrifice for our family moving forward, battling with all my might to go and see Trina and my son a couple of weeks after his birth. When we met up, I was devastated to hear about the difficulty of his birth, including the concern at times that I could have lost one or both of them. The stories Trina told about her pregnancy and giving birth to my son were scary, hard to hear, especially since I felt disappointed I wasn't there to help. The only fact that made listening to her story easier was that I knew the ending, that both had made it through and were healthy. But my son wouldn't come to me. Every time Trina gave him to me, he began to scream and push me away. It was very heartbreaking that the whole weekend we visited he wanted nothing to do with this stranger. I couldn't help my thoughts drifting to growing up in a single-parent home, wondering if me not being there while he grew was going to cause him as much pain. I knew at that moment that I'd sacrificed too much already and found a new gear to make sure there was no chance I wouldn't be successful and graduate. I went back to Depot and powered through everything to make it to the graduation day and ceremony. That day I'd be the highest I'd been in my life. I'd become a police officer, had found my dream wife, my dream family, and now had my dream job. It was the first time I'd entered a career, not just a job, starting my forever employment and making decent money to support my family in a manner I'd never been able to do before. I felt on that day that I'd sacrificed and faced some adversity, but had overcome all that and life was about to be a dream realized.

Chapter Six - When Dreams Become Nightmares

There I was, finally living the dream, and I truly was. Everything was going right and I truly felt on top of the world. The only problem was that would leave an awful long way to fall. The first day I showed up to work, I was like the most excited kid on the first day of school ever. I quickly realized that even though training had done a great job of preparing me for my career, they weren't able to prepare me for everything that I'd potentially face. That's why the profession of policing pairs brand new recruits with an experienced officer, someone who can show them the ropes and help them learn the application of the knowledge they acquire in training. I learned a lot of applications, from all of the members of the detachment, and having so many different personalities really allowed me to find my way as well. However, just as the baby bird has to fly on his own, so does the newly hired member leave the safety of their experienced field trainer, So there I was, on my own shift, in my own car, doing the job myself. What I remember most about that time was the excitement. Everything was new and everything was exciting. I went home every night so full of life and joy. At some point in time, I became what I believed was experienced. In fact, I was so experienced that I wasn't excited. Each call began to blur into every other. I struggled a lot with my decision at that point. I'd sacrificed so much, knowing that this was my dream job with so much variety I couldn't possibly get bored in a million years. Yet there I was, not even a year into my career, and I was beginning to get bored. It hadn't taken long for my career to become just a job, paying the bills. I wasn't sure if I was making any difference in the world, or certainly not the difference I'd intended to make at the outset.

 I found that not only was work not exciting to me, but things at home weren't exciting either. Every once in a while, my son would do something that would surprise me, or my daughter would do something that amazed me, but these were only glimmers in an otherwise pretty mundane world. I needed to simply go home and turn off the world, just forget that everything else existed. I began to find a bunch of computer games I enjoyed playing, just silly little games about owning restaurants or things like that. I'd get home on my time off and get lost in these games for hours or even days, although they didn't excite me either, merely allowing me to shut off all of my thinking. I didn't have the energy to parent. I just wanted to have fun and the time I did spend with the kids I just wanted to be fun, not involving disciplining or correcting their behaviour, but sadly most of my fun was with my games. I didn't have much time for fun with the children, or indeed much time for anything in those days. I was lost in the games or at work analyzing my decision. Were the sacrifices worth it? Why did my job and life suck, and also suck the life out of me? I spent time with a couple of acquaintances, complaining about how much I hated work. I realized by that point that I detested work. Every day was worse than the day before and I felt being on call was keeping me so busy, I had no time for anything else. What was the point of all that sacrifice if I didn't have any time to do anything? My life had become so hectic. Even though I only lived a few blocks from work, I didn't even have time to go home for lunch. Instead, on every workday I found myself eating at least one of my meals at a restaurant. Not only was the perceived lack of time affecting what I could do on my day, the thought of being called out was affecting my sleep. I mostly laid awake, just expecting the phone to ring, and most of those call-outs were to a traumatic event of some kind. I found it hard to sleep much more than a couple of hours a night. With no sleep, no time, a job I hated, and a diet that didn't make my body feel good, I was becoming increasingly frustrated. By the time I arrived home I was always near my boiling point, one spill, one thing not going my way, away from losing my temper and yelling at someone. I knew something had gone wrong in my life. I was no longer the person I had been, but I was confused because I hadn't changed. I'd become angry with everyone around me, angry at myself, and didn't like this person I was. I'd zone out in those games, thinking about what went wrong, where it had gone wrong, and how I could get back to being that person I'd been growing up, so full of laughter, life, and love.

I needed to figure out how to get back to being that person. When did I last feel or see that person? I knew I was still that person at Depot, but I couldn't go back to being a cadet, so I'd have to go back further. I looked at my fondest childhood memories and realized they revolved around fitness and martial arts. I was very surprised when I reflected on the previous year and a bit, realizing that at the time I did neither of those things. I couldn't find a worthwhile gym or a place to train martial arts in the town I lived. I also didn't have that kind of time, so I turned my basement into a gym and martial art area. After all, I didn't need to learn martial arts. Just doing them should take me back to where I was. I hung a heavy bag, got a kettlebell, and was set to be able to work out and train some martial arts. Of course, the major problem was finding the time and there wasn't a lot of that to spare. I also didn't have a lot of energy to start a workout, so sometimes I'd just start with my games. However, that usually ended up as a day of playing the games and nothing more. I realized that as long as I was directing my training, it was going to be intermittent at best. I had to get to where I'd be committed, somewhere I was expected to be, so I found an internal martial art called Jiulong Bauguzhang in Saskatoon and started attending weekend seminars. I was immediately impressed with the skill shown there and began to make classes once in a while, when I wasn't too tired or busy. It was at these classes that I learnt a type of meditation simply referred to as quiet sitting. I don't know what it was but when I did fifteen minutes a day, my problems seemed to be insignificant, or at least less significant. I was very faithful in my practice and thing were going well. I seemed calmer and had more room to deal with spills and unexpected events. I still found the job really hard though. I felt like I was trapped after asking my family to sacrifice so much. How could I tell them I no longer wanted to be a police officer? I was good at practicing quiet sitting on my own for about six months, but then I just was too tired, too exhausted, and needed to use that time to sleep. I missed for many reasons and very quickly fell out of practice.

One night I'd get a call that would change my life. It was the most dangerous call that I'd dealt with up to that point in my career. It was so dangerous that as an officer that had never called for back up, I found myself screaming into the microphone, calling for help. When I was informed that no one local could be reached and the nearest car was forty minutes away, my heart sank and I knew I was on my own for at least forty minutes. I weighed all the options, but relied heavily on my training to guide me. When back-up finally arrived, we were able to bring the situation to a peaceful resolution and I continued with my night. It had been one of the few occasions when there had been an excitement that I wasn't used to feeling. However, I had no ambition to recreate that excitement. The very next time my mother saw me after that night, she commented on how much I'd changed. Nothing that I was doing to become myself again was working, which ended up being one factor in the decision to move services. I knew something was wrong and thought that maybe it was because of the service, not the job. Perhaps I wasn't wrong after all. Maybe it was still my dream job. I just needed to stop being on call then I wouldn't be tired all the time and could eat and feel better.

     I moved to Saskatoon Police Service, excited that I wasn't going to have the fear of being transferred over my head, I wasn't going to have to be on call, and with four days on, four days off, I expected to be a brand new person. Although the process to get hired still required the same steps as when I was first hired as a police officer, it was a much easier process as I was already in a good-paying job that was supporting my family and didn't have any goals to get a different job. When I was hired I was excited to see that I was right. All I had needed was a change of service and then the job, the profession, excited me so much again, and with no on-call status I could enjoy my days off. Of course, in the beginning, I was placed with an experienced officer again, to show me the processes that their service used. As with any two companies, there were some procedural changes to learn. Once I was back on my own, except for partners during the evening shifts, this new excitement and enthusiasm for the industry lasted for about a year. I found myself having the same problems. I couldn't sleep, but of course, that was simply because now I had to drive an hour to work and an hour back home, so that extra time gave me less time to sleep. Because I had less time to sleep, I had no time to make my lunches and continued to eat a diet that didn't make my body feel great, but it was fast and worked with the time I had. I was losing energy by the minute and again began to feel trapped. The time I was sleeping I was having nightmares and I was embarrassed that, as an adult, I was having those. The daytime wasn't much better. I was haunted by images that I couldn't shake from my mind and found myself watching around every corner, everywhere I went, expecting to see death, whether it was at the grocery store or a large crowded event. I could never get away from these feelings and kept feeling worse and worse, mentally and physically. I knew that I had to overcome those emotions. That's when the idea popped in my head, that I needed to become immune to emotions and not feel them anymore.

One day I went to a call that was a related to what I'd imagine would be a very traumatic event for most people. I was able to do all of my work without wavering. Afterward, I even reassured myself.

"You've done it. You're so emotionless now, you've beaten emotions."

I wondered why everyone else hadn't done this. I'd hear family members and friends that were upset about events in their lives, or incidents they had observed I couldn't understand how they could be that way, so emotional. I thought that if they'd seen what I'd seen, they wouldn't be complaining. I can only imagine the coldness I portrayed to friends and family. Throughout this whole time, I still cared for people. I wanted to be the best father, husband, and employee I could be, but I was also fighting some limited resources of energy. I always seemed burnt out for some reason. One night I went to a traumatic call with a new partner. To me, it was business as usual. I'd been to this type of call many times before. The next night my partner explained that after going home, she'd cried because of the event. The very first response in my head was the phrase 'cops don't cry' but I put that aside and listened, attempting to help my partner as best as I could. However, I was having more and more trouble understanding emotions and why people were upset. I went to another call that would be classified as traumatic and shortly after finishing,

I received a call from the staff sergeant. He was wanting to make sure I was okay, offering the opportunity to talk to someone about it, if I needed. I thanked the staff sergeant for their concern, but stated that I was fine. I didn't need to talk and explained that it had been business as usual. I thought it was so great that I'd found a way to completely overcome emotions. However, life was getting tougher and tougher. I felt miles apart from my family, even though we lived in the same house. In my mind I felt further away than when I was training at Depot in Saskatchewan and they were back in BC. Even though I'd defeated emotions, I couldn't get the images to stop playing in my mind. I couldn't get the nightmares to stop either.

I began to doubt myself, along with the decisions I made and the person I was. I started to wonder what was wrong with me. Why was I the only one in the world having these issues? Why was I having nightmares as an adult? I was even having daymares too. And it felt as if I was always yelling at my family. What was wrong with me? I used to be so exceptional at my job, but at the time I was barely adequate. I was aware that the mental cycle continued regularly, and perhaps constantly, and I was unaware. On every drive to work, and every drive home, I found myself wondering what would happen if I just kept on driving. What if instead of stopping for work I just kept going, until my car ran out of gas and I found some secluded area, where I could live in isolation for the rest of my life. I wanted everything to stop. People were always pushing my buttons and making me angry. I didn't like the person I'd become. I liked the me who was calm, not some angry person. Maybe living in isolation was the solution. I followed this train of thought for quite some time until finally, I'd think about how my family would react to me leaving and never coming back. When I thought about their sadness, I knew I had to keep pushing on. Yet the thoughts of continuing to drive and find a place of isolation continued. I also found myself sitting in my car before or after my shift. I'd look down at my gun and begin a train of thought.

"I wonder how easy it would be to just end it all? If I did a proper trigger pull with no anticipation, by the time I knew the gun was going to go off, it would all be over."

Again, it would be when I thought about my family and them being upset that I'd return to the realization that I had to keep pushing on.

During this time, I was still only getting at best four or five hours of sleep any given night, whether I was working or had a day off. I couldn't find the time to make my lunch and began to eat all three meals on a workday at some kind of fast food place. I was spending up to $570 a month on fast food. This silly spending was causing financial strain and creating friction with Trina. Every week I'd assure her that I knew how much I'd spent the previous week, but would try hard to be way better. However, when the workday rolled around, I couldn't find the energy to make a healthy lunch. I had many justifications about why it had to be that way. It wasn't my fault, I had to drive an hour each way to work, I had a busy workday, or there was no other choice. It was a very conflicted time. I blamed and shamed myself for how I was, but placed an equal amount of blame on the external factors that were the problem. Each day became more and more of a struggle and just getting out of bed became an arduous task. Still, I continued to push on, trying to figure out what was wrong, what was causing my thoughts and actions. I started to focus heavily on the job being the problem. After all, I knew me before I'd become a police officer, and I knew me now. The only explanation for my change in behaviour had to be police work. I started to focus on all the negative things related to my career, such as the shift work that was messing with my sleep patterns, or the unpredictable workday that had caused me to have to eat at restaurants on a regular basis. At that moment, I knew the solution was simple. All I had to do was find a way to no longer work in policing. I spent money on every little course I could find, hoping that each one would allow me to go into business for myself, because that would eliminate all the problems that I was facing. However, each new course just led to me needing another course and I wasn't making any money at trying to provide services based on any of these courses. I'd done courses like hot stone massage, but providing the massages was just too exhausting, especially for an already exhausted person. One day I decided to contact a friend and find out how he'd been able to leave the police service. I wondered how it worked and what situation or circumstance had caused him to be off work, yet still get paid. I knew it was something medical but nothing I was familiar with. We sat down for dinner and he told me he had Post Traumatic Stress Disorder (PTSD). I asked him what that was and how he'd been diagnosed with it. He relayed a story of a traumatic call he'd attended, to which I could relate. I'd attended several very similar calls. I began to wonder if a doctor had diagnosed him with PTSD from just one event and if that was my problem. I can honestly say I'd never even considered that I might have PTSD. I knew nothing about it, but I hoped my doctor would be able to enlighten me. About two days after my conversation with my friend, I went to my doctor. I was then off on medical leave and required to see a psychologist. I have to admit that I didn't believe in psychologists. How was it possible for them to know what was going on in my mind? They couldn't see that and they also hadn't lived through what I had. I knew I was going to the psychologist reluctantly.

I originally wrote this chapter with a focus on the specific events that occurred in my career that had turned this dream job into a nightmare. However, as my recovery went better and better,

I realized the events were never important. Everyone responds to stressors differently and has different events that will stress them, so it doesn't matter what the specific stresses were. More important were the signs I missed, the unhealthy behaviours I developed, the ability to keep finding justifications for all the behaviours, including the thoughts of ending it all, and finally the learning that occurred, the reaching out to a friend able to share knowledge of a similar situation and condition, which would ultimately get me on the correct track to seek and find the help I'd need.

Chapter Seven - Getting Help

The time had come and I was seeing a psychologist. I didn't know how they could help me. I still wasn't convinced that the psychologist did anything, but I had to go. At the very first session I was very reserved as we did our introductions, before he began asking me questions. I didn't want to give him too much, still thinking that the entire process was pointless. He asked a question that I hesitated to answer and as he pressed me for details. Since that was getting us nowhere, he explained why he needed to know and the information that he was trying to gather. It was at that moment that I realized how much the psychologist might actually know about what was going on in my mind. I'd missed this sign, dismissing it as insignificant. I'd stopped playing any video games that involved shooting. I had tons of favourite games that I used to play, but at some point I'd just stopped and went to the silly games about owning restaurants or businesses. Then I started to tell him about some of the experiences that had caused me distress. I was telling the story about waiting for backup when suddenly something unusual and unfamiliar happened to me.

I began to feel liquid coming out of my eyes, my breathing became difficult, and I struggled to speak. I couldn't believe that I was crying. I could only remember one previous occasion when I'd cried, about a week after my grandfather passed away, but my grandfather had taken the place of my father wherever he could. Even then, I only cried one or two tears and moved on, as crying wouldn't bring him back. Yet there I was, crying uncontrollably, without stopping.

I left the office, fairly certain I was never going back. I had a second appointment booked, but wasn't sure how I could return and look my psychologist in the face after crying in his office. The sense of embarrassment I felt was unbelievable. Of course, I had to return. It was my job now, so I'd barely sat down in his office before I apologized.

"I'm sorry I cried the last session. I don't know what was wrong, I'm so embarrassed."

The psychologist seemed unfazed and accepted my crying as normal behaviour. That moment was one of the biggest ones on my road to recovery. It would help me to understand that all the reactions I'd had to the traumatic events I witnessed were normal human responses to abnormal situations. I felt like I wasn't broken, but I'd been fighting against myself, trying to suppress the natural responses of my body and mind. I hadn't beaten emotions. I'd only been suppressing them, which caused the body to start hurting at a level where it would get my attention in ways I couldn't ignore. These included gaining so much weight, becoming lethargic and struggling to get out of bed, increased anger, self-isolation, avoidance of places that reminded me of events, and thoughts of wanting it all to end. After that session, I was diagnosed with severe PTSD.

I don't recall the content of every single session I had with the psychologist. I do remember making sure that he understood that I could never go back to work again, not to policing and not to the service. I had severe PTSD, which sounded really bad and I didn't want to have severe PTSD ever again. At one point, he finally shut that down.

"Look," he said. "We're going to deal with the PTSD and you'll have a choice to go back and will make a decision like an adult."

Once he said this I spent many hours trying to determine how it could be true. How could I get better? And even if I got better, how could I get better to the point where I could start seeing and responding to events that might cause issues to resurface? And even if all of those other things were true and did happen, how could I ever go to the police station again, after years of not performing my job at the level I once had. Sure, at the time it was the best I could do, but that was far from what I'd been capable of before the PTSD. And to make matters worse, I was off of work, putting additional strain on everyone else who now also had to pick up my work. Another concern was how I could show my face, considering what people were probably saying about me. I never heard anything but felt that the general conversation would be about how I was faking an injury that no one could see, just so I could be off work. How would my co-workers treat me when I returned? I knew the decision I'd have to make when that time came.

I kept attending sessions and began to feel lighter and lighter. I hadn't even realized I'd been carrying a heavy emotional load until it began to disappear and I could note the contrast. By then I was back training internal martial arts. One day during the Baguazhang class we were training outside and doing a standing meditation, where we'd stand in good structure and hold various poses. Since it was a public park, every time I opened my eyes it felt like the people I saw were watching us, watching us intently.

"Don't worry about what anyone else is thinking about you," the instructor said to everyone. "Or more importantly, don't worry about what you think they're thinking about you, because you don't know and it doesn't matter."

That hit me like a bolt of lightning. It didn't matter what others thought of me, and more importantly, how could I truly know. Even their body language wasn't enough to give complete insight into what they were thinking. We were learning to just be in that moment, doing what we were doing, and not chasing silly thoughts like speculating what the people passing by were thinking of us. At that time, I also had the most life-changing session with the psychologist. I arrived at his office as usual and the sessions had become my most enjoyable part of my week.

"Do you know what mindfulness is?" my psychologist asked.

"Of course I do," I responded.

"Good," he said. "Because I think that's something you need to think about. None of these situations causing you distress are happening at this moment."

He then began to explain about mindfulness and provide me with some techniques. I guess he wanted to make sure I truly understood mindfulness. I left the office for my hour drive home and began to feel concerned. I had no idea what he was talking about regarding mindfulness. I just didn't want to be the guy who didn't know something that I figured must be so obvious to every one else, because of how often I'd heard the term used. I knew I'd have to figure out what this mindfulness was before the next session, because I was sure he was going to ask about it.

I embarked on an online journey to learn everything I could about mindfulness, what it was, and how to do it. I found an eight-week course on becoming a mindfulness instructor and knew I had to learn the technique. I first began to assess all the moments of my life where I wasn't mindful and was amazed to find my day was full of them. Most of the reactions I was having at places like the grocery store were due to the moments where my mind would wander. I'd scan the store looking for the 'bad person', someone who was there to harm me in some way. What kind of attack were they going to launch? Would they have a weapon? Would I have to defend myself or others? Before I knew it, my body would respond in the same way as if I was in an actual life or death situation. My fist would clench, my body would fill with adrenaline, and I was ready for fight or flight. I wasn't being mindful, so my thoughts were taking me to a situation that wasn't actually happening. During the course, I learnt many techniques to help me become more mindful, both in general and when I was having a specific experience. One of the most shocking revelations was that I'd already learned many of these techniques through various martial arts and just not realized it.

One of the simplest techniques became my favourite, focusing on the breath, the most mindful thing we already do. As long as we continue to breathe, most people find it very difficult to focus on a breath they are about to have, or one they previously had. Instead they find their mind drawn immediately to the breath they're currently taking. I was certainly unable to focus on a future or past breath, only on previous occasion when I couldn't breathe at all like choking or occasions where I had difficulty breathing, laboured breathing like an asthma attack. The truly important part of this newfound mindfulness was awareness. I had to be aware when my mind began to trail off, focusing on past or potential future events, then employ mindfulness. I began to challenge myself to go to public places, starting with easy ones like the grocery store. In the beginning, it would only take a few moments before my mind would start to ask the questions, preparing for a life or death situation, but then I'd remember to focus on my breath, not change it just focus on it. I'd forget about all the other thoughts as I began to observe my breath, how deep it was, and where the air was entering and exiting. I'd think about where the air was going in my body, plus what the temperature was when it entered or left. Almost instantly my hands would unclench, my shoulders would drop, my breathing would become deeper, and my body and mind would relax. I can't remember the day I stopped having to think about focusing on mindfulness, but it did become an instant process that I never had to consciously think about. I began to challenge myself to go to more and more places. Once I conquered one, I challenged myself to go to the next. When I could go to the grocery store like every other person, I wondered if I could eat in a restaurant in an area of the city that previously caused me distress. I eventually got to the stage where I could go to a fair or a concert, with many strangers, and have a relaxing day dealing with what actually happened, which of course bore little resemblance to anything my mind had imagined.

I continued my sessions with the psychologist and he helped me to rationalize, understand what had happened, and how I had dealt with it. He helped me to understand the importance of dealing with these situations in a healthy manner. He brought perspective into my life and helped me to normalize both the events and my responses to them. I went off work in February 2014 and the following September I returned to work, with modified hours and duties. The very first day was probably the most uneasy one of my professional career. I was more nervous than my first day as a cadet in training, wondering how people would respond. However, I was armed with the power of mindfulness and could always remember what my instructor had said that day we'd practiced outside.

"More importantly don't worry about what you think they're thinking about you."

Old friends greeted me just as they always had, which really helped me settle back into a routine. People that didn't know me well did treat me differently. They treated me as if I was a person made of glass, fragile ready to break at any moment. Others wouldn't include me in any of the back and forth mocking that goes onto between groups of good friends. This wasn't because they didn't wish to include me in the group, but because they feared it would harm me more than someone else.

The hardest part of my return was the misconception about PTSD and what it meant. In my learning, I equated the psychological injury of PTSD to a physical injury. You get injured, seek professional help, and then learn strategies to strengthen the body from harm should a similar situation occur. I made sure that I was always open and never embarrassed to tell people why I was off. I'd tell everyone who asked that I'd been diagnosed with severe PTSD. The most amazing aspect of my return was regaining my ability to work. Finally, I'd reached a point where I was able to do exceptional work again. I was no longer overwhelmed by the stress that had built in my life. I was able to do my job, foresee and predict problems, and devise solutions to deal with them. I continued to work on and develop skills in my life that helped me to reduce stress and prevent it from building. I used skills like mindfulness, which lead me to explore tai chi and qigong, martial arts that spent a great deal of time focusing on mindfulness in motion. I recognized that prior to being away from work, I'd never been willing to discuss anything that bothered me, at least not with anyone I knew. I developed a good support network, utilizing my lifelong friend, Lyle, so that I had an outlet in which to vent. I'd previously struggled with the concept of privacy, as well as being able to vent or choosing not to vent at all. However, during this time I also realized that simply saying I saw something that bothered me was enough, that to release the event didn't require me to explain in detail what the event was. I just had to acknowledge that it bothered me and choose to let it go. I also utilized a technique of clearing in tai chi to feel a physical release of the tension in my body. However, due to modified duties, I hadn't really been able to test my skills in the fire, so to speak. I began to challenge myself slowly, increasingly immersing myself in more aspects of work, allowing myself to slowly get used to using those techniques.

The Workers Compensation Board (WCB) required me to provide them with details of specific traumatic situations, ones that would have caused PTSD. As I was going back through them, I remembered a very traumatic situation that had led me to believe I'd beat my emotions. I began crying, quickly leaving the building so that no one would see me. I then texted Lyle to let him know that thinking about past experiences had caused me to cry. His response was that it was good and the experience I'd witnessed was something that I probably should have wept about at the time. The conversation really helped me to validate a couple of thoughts, Firstly, my support group didn't have to know about the event to support me so I could keep my privacy oath, and secondly, emotions were normal. I came to the further understanding that the phrase 'cops don't cry' had misled me and caused me to keep burying my emotional response to the traumatic calls I attended, caused me to emotionally build up until I couldn't handle the feelings by myself. I then realized that to offer assistance during a traumatic event, I may have to set emotions aside temporarily in order to complete the task of helping the people involved, but I must always acknowledge the emotions. In that sense, the expression should perhaps have been that cops cry later.

As I continued to challenge and learn, I didn't quite feel right. I was working but not doing the job I'd agreed to do. I knew that I had to keep pushing and challenging myself until I could get cleared for active duty. However, Trina had some reservations and didn't want me to start the process to get cleared for regular duty. I understood what she'd gone through. She'd usually borne the brunt of my verbal outbursts. She was the person that had to pick up my duties when I became too tired to parent properly. She'd had to deal with my self-isolation, not being willing to go anywhere except my own house. Once I was working again, and not having these problems, I suspect that her biggest fear was that active duty would take me back down that road. I gave her some time to explore whatever options she needed to help her move forward, such as her seeing a psychologist or however she wanted to prepare for me beginning the process of returning to active duty. In early 2016, I started seeing the psychologist to begin the process to be cleared for duty. By the summer of 2016, I was completely cleared of all restrictions and back to active duty, where I remain at the time of writing this book in 2020.

Chapter Eight - Aftermath

When people hear my story, they often have one main question. They wonder whether I was as good when I returned as I'd ben before I left.

"No," I reply each time, before adding after a short pause, "I'm a million times better now than I ever was."

When I first started my career in policing, I hadn't seen a lot of personal trauma. Yes, I'd had challenges in my life but hadn't been subjected to an unusual amount of traumatic situations. I'd acquired the ability to block out physical pain, as I'd done with the wasp that was stinging me. I naively believed that I could also overcome emotional pain in a similar way, by just choosing to ignore it. This belief had caused me to ignore my emotions and suppress them during every traumatic call I attended. Of course, by ignoring them, they manifested in other ways to get my attention, by showing up as nightmares or flashbacks that I referred to as daymares. I've since modified this belief. I can still focus on tasks during a traumatic situation, but I always go back to acknowledge the emotions. One day, I was thinking about being back for the last four years, more time than it had originally taken me to develop PTSD. Had I really challenged my skills with a traumatic situation? Or had I just had an easier four years than I'd experienced at the beginning of my career? What would happen if I did attend a traumatic event, would the skills I had learned work for a traumatic call? I thought about the years since my return in 2016 and couldn't remember a single event that had been traumatic. I suddenly began laughing when I realized I had been to one, just a couple of weeks before. However, after the call I went back and acknowledged the emotional toll it had taken on me and released the call and the emotions. By doing that I couldn't remember the traumatic elements of the call, even a couple of weeks later. The call, situation, and required task I could recall in complete detail. However, it didn't flag in my mind as traumatic until I thoroughly thought about the call, because of what I did afterward to deal with the emotions. This knowledge that I'm human, and will have normal responses to abnormal situations, is a huge piece of information to prevent me from being blindsided. I'll no longer make the mistake of thinking that just because I am able to pause my emotions to perform my duties, to pause my emotions to be able to help others in their time of need, that I can in fact pause my emotions indefinitely, but instead I recognize that I must unpause and deal with the emotions properly as soon as practicable. I know that it was never PTSD that had deceived me, but me deceiving myself. I'm now aware that by suppressing emotions, burying them, and viewing such a technique as a success, I failed to recognize the danger I was in by not addressing the stress. I also failed to recognize the growing danger. Going forward, with the acknowledgment that I'll have an emotional toll to deal with, allows me to never fool myself into building up my emotions, where I just can't deal with it anymore. This also makes me a better person day to day. Now a spill can be just a spill, while an unexpected event can be an interesting challenge because my emotional bucket is no longer always filled to the top.

    The second thing that makes me a million times better are the daily routines I've built into my life that I never had before. These routines allow me to deal with the regular stressors of life, keeping me centered and calm. I tell myself to engage in my routines when I'm feeling stressed and double my routines when I'm feeling great. I'm aware that I stray away from my helpful routines in life when I'm feeling great. I then get so far away from my healthy habits that life becomes chaotic, so that starting those healthy routines can be extremely hard, even though I know they'd be helpful. Having my daily routines is an important part of my continued success. I observed in the past, while suffering from PTSD, that things like quiet sitting didn't help me when I needed it the most. Why was this? The simple answer was that I stopped doing the quiet sitting as I begin to feel good. I'd then get to a place so overwhelmed that I no longer had the energy to perform the simple task. The same is true with physical exercise. The body doesn't continue to produce results when I stop working out for months at a time, yet I'd expected or been willfully blind to the fact that would be the case when I stopped my emotional exercise. Going forward, I know just how important physical and mental exercise is to my home health, personal health, and work health. I recognize the importance of having daily habits designed to help relieve physical and mental stress, even if I don't observe it currently in my life. Having these daily routines is going to be hugely important going forward with my career, to avoid becoming overwhelmed. This is because I won't be attempting to put routines in place at the moment where I'm already overwhelmed by life in general, let alone wanting to add something new. Through my experiences with PTSD comes the knowledge that I know I have to practice daily so that the routines become habits, that I just naturally do, that they have become ingrained while I feel healthy and while I fell I am not emotionally overwhelmed, and I'm aware that I also have to implement them incrementally so that I don't overwhelm the body and mind. Once I get either a physical or mental routine established, I then begin to look at the addition of a new one. I've also learned to recognize the importance of implementing daily routines that I enjoy. By having daily routines for physical and mental fitness in place, I'm better equipped to deal with stress in my life, helping to prevent suffering from PTSD.

The third thing that makes me a million times better is knowing the enemy, I not only know what PTSD looked like in my life at its worst, but also what it looked like step-by-step. In martial arts, I was always taught to be successful in a defense. I needed to know myself and my enemy. I previously had no idea of what the PTSD monster looked like. In fact, I truly felt it was just a mythical monster, certainly not something that would ever affect my life. I was unable to fight the enemy when I didn't know or recognize it was there. Instead, I fooled myself with justifications for behaviours or delusion about events. Trying to explain my life at that point, with known causes. I'd justified my junk food eating habits using time as an excuse. I didn't have the time to eat healthily. I was just being a team player but going out to breakfast or lunch. I was aware that time management could be an issue with me and, of course, I had the reality of an additional two hours added on to my workday. It was really easy to justify my junk food behaviour by blaming time management, something I knew to be a problem. I'd displace the blame for my anger. Anger wasn't a problem I had. Rather, it was everyone around me, as they sought to push buttons and make me mad. This was another easy scapegoat. Many people had told me that certain points in a marriage are hard, such as the second year, the seventh year, the fifteenth year. Many people also had told me that raising children was the toughest job they ever did. I found these two ideas to be easy scapegoats and thus I didn't need to look any harder to find a problem. I'd blame my workplace for my frustration there, even though I'd changed organizations and still had the same issue. Blaming work was easy. After all, they call it work for a reason and work isn't referred to as fun. These days, I'm on high alert for the PTSD monster and know that it might disguise itself as the issues above. That knowledge comes from the ability to see life after PTSD and realize I love 99 percent of interactions with my wife and children. Marriage takes work but it's not hard. Trina's my best friend and who doesn't like hanging out with their best friend. Raising my children naturally presents some challenges, but those pale in comparison to the joy and fulfillment the children bring. I'm able to see and feel that today when I'm not in a stressed state. I know to watch out for the excuses to isolate myself. My workplace still has challenges, but I can honestly say I find more joy than frustration during a working day. I'm able to have that hindsight view that it was never the workplace causing distress, but the events at work that I was ignoring. Although PTSD became a huge monster it was actually a little monster ignored, which I unknowingly continued to feed it until it became huge and unmanageable. I'm armed with the knowledge as I continue to move forward, to recognize the little changes, utilize my support systems, and assess whether it's just a bad day like we all have or something more serious that I need to address. I make sure to keep a watch when I'm low on energy or not wanting to go somewhere. I make sure I understand the reason why so I don't get tricked into little unhealthy changes in my life. I know the importance of seeking professional help as soon as possible, because I was able to witness the powerful effects a psychologist could have on my life at such a low point. Yes, I know the enemy, I know the disguise he or she might use, and know the tricks my mind will employ to ignore the monster. Consequently, I'm now at a stage in my life where I shouldn't be fooled again.

The fourth thing that makes me a million times better is knowing the importance of a support group, as well as understanding how to vent without revealing information I've promised to keep secret. For many years, I experienced a tough battle alone because I didn't want to harm anyone else along the way. Instead of sharing a traumatic event even with my colleagues, I chose to keep it to myself. Their jobs were already hard enough and they didn't need my stress too. I should have caught this factor much earlier in my career, as a bunch of us had got together with members from another detachment. At some point, the conversation became about food aversion after traumatic calls we'd attended. One officer shared that after a certain call he could never eat bacon. I was so relieved to hear this, for the previous year I'd been embarrassed that

I could no longer eat chow mein. It was a dish I loved. My brother Justin and I even loved to go to the grocery store to buy the ingredients. I also loved chow mein when eating out, but I never could again after I attended the scene. However I was far too embarrassed to mention that to anyone. Not only did I believe I was the only one in the world with that issue, I also had no idea what the connection was between food and traumatic event not involving food at all. Even though it was relief to feel normal when I realized that others in my situation were having the same reactions, that was the last one of those talks I ever had. I now realize the importance of sharing and releasing those stresses, but I'm also more aware of what resources are available to me, provided through my workplace or outside of it. Understanding the importance of speaking with others, what resources are available, and understanding that call stressors can be discussed without providing details of the calls, has made me prepared to deal with all future traumatic events. I now have the foresight to not refuse help or fail to attend a critical incident stress debriefing. Going forward, this helps me to not allow a traumatic incident to linger and grow.

The fifth thing that makes me a million times better today is my understanding of the importance of being non-judgemental. My issues with PTSD started with judgments, such as those about the type of people who would be affected by such an injury. These included judgments about what PTSD would look like, how obvious it would be, and what people would think of me if I reached out to get help. There were also judgments about myself, both for being afflicted with PTSD and the behavioural and life results in a state where I was extremely overwhelmed and stressed out. I started my journey with forgiveness. I truly had to forgive myself for the judgments I made about what type of people I'd thought could or would be affected by PTSD. I was able to humble myself by recognizing just how easy it was for anyone to be affected. I had to forgive myself for the signs I missed and remember to not pass judgment. I can never honestly say if someone else in my situation would have caught the signs earlier and it really doesn't matter, because I didn't and can accept and learn from it. I now heavily rely on not trying to guess how others are judging me. More importantly, I accept that everyone has an opinion and although it's important to listen to all perspectives, I don't need to fit the mold that everyone else thinks is ideal for me. I have to be able to return home, proud of myself, proud of the person I choose to be, and not worry about what someone else might think is right for me. I spent years avoiding even thinking about getting help. Even if I hadn't recognized the problem, I knew there was a problem, but refused to seek help for fear of what others might think. I'm now able to realize that others likely thought a lot less of me for not asking for help. This was primarily because I performed as a person and employee far below the level at which I perform when I'm not overwhelmed by stress. I'm armed with the knowledge that it will always be easy for others to judge me, but I must accept and hear their judgments only where their judgments can assist me to be better, to improve myself, otherwise their judgments must simply be ignored. It would be hard for them to understand the full picture unless they truly knew me as my support people do. I had to forgive myself and for what I believed to be many years of failure. I feel as though I failed my wife, my family, my employees, and most importantly, myself. Looking back on that time, I recognize that I can never take those years back, but it only becomes a true failure if I choose not to learn from it. I make the choice of seeing it as not a failure but a key to my success. When my daughter saw a short blog post I'd written about PTSD for a website, she came over crying and hugged me, upset that she'd never realized what I was going through. By not judging myself as being bad, I can accept ownership of my actions, except that my choice to learn from my experience and deal with any future stress before it becomes a problem will be what defines me, not a misstep I had on my journey to knowledge. By forgiving myself and accepting my actions with others, I'm able to move forward, not as though it never happened, but with forgiveness that we all make mistakes. The ability to be non-judgmental helps in moving forward too, as I no longer have judgments clouding my observations. I can just observe my responses to my life and make decisions for my best health. Even if I don't like that a call bothers me, I can accept that it does and deal with the stress before it becomes too large to handle. Non-judgment of ourselves and others goes a long way to building our self-confidence as well.

These five skills that I've learned have made me a million times better today in my personal and professional life. I say that I'm the husband I always wanted to be, the father I always wanted to be, and the employee I wanted to be. This is all wrapped in the knowledge that all of these areas are growing too. As I stumble and learn I'm able to become better in all aspects of my life. Each and every day I become better and that's an important point to remember, that when we're able to keep our stress managed we can grow, and I hope to continue to grow as well as learn.

I hope that sharing my story inspires any of those that are suffering to realize there is a wonderful light at the end of the tunnel. It takes work, and the work will always be there, but the work is worth every ounce of joy and peace it provides. I hope that sharing the lessons I've learned reminds people of the importance of kindness. We never know what people are dealing with, and judging them today may be a gross error regarding who they are, or may become. I hope this book is a reminder that none of us have to suffer alone and that we shouldn't suffer in silence. There are people who can help. There are people who have walked a similar road and would love to provide some guidance to help make your journey a little easier.

About The Author

Jason Rorick

Jason has been a martial artist from the age of 10 years old, where he learned many great lessons in the art of perseverance in the face of adversity. His love for martial arts and the journey in this book, lead him to become a mindfulness meditation instructor and Clears Qigong instructor. Jason has also always had a love for language which encouraged him to become trained as a Master Neural Linguistic Practitioner.

Made in the USA
Columbia, SC
30 December 2020